Fifty Shades of Rubber Stamping:
A 'how-to' guide with step-by-step instructions

Fifty Shades of Rubber Stamping:
A 'how-to' guide with step-by-step instructions

by Amanda Bartlett

This book contains fifty different ways of rubber stamping. I have designed it to be used as a reference guide for different techniques, and each technique has a project with it. So, the book can be used to refer to a particular technique, as well as an ideas book for projects to make. There are projects for both beginners and more experienced stampers so there is something for everyone.

Amanda's Homecrafts
2013

Acknowledgments

I would like to thank my wonderful husband who does all the technical things for me, my children who are very tolerant of my crafting taking over everywhere, my Mum and friends who have been 'tea ladies', Stampin' Up!, whose products inspire me, and fellow demonstrators who share their love of rubber stamping. I would especially like to thank all my ladies who have enjoyed crafting with me, whose company is lovely, and who have encouraged me to write this book. Crafting has given me such pleasure, and I've made some wonderful friendships through it, which to me is what crafting is really all about.

Visit the Amanda's Homecrafts website at www.amandashomecrafts.com for monthly projects, Stampin' Up! news, product reviews and more.

About the Author

Amanda has enjoyed various crafts, and particularly rubber stamping as a hobby for approximately twenty years. She enjoys sharing what she loves with other people in the form of workshops, and is also an independent Stampin' Up! demonstrator. She lives in Warwickshire with her husband and two sons.

Stampin' Up!

The projects have been designed by the author and are not a product of Stampin' Up!. Stampin' Up! products can be ordered through your nearest demonstrator (check on line).

Any items made using Stampin' Up! products that are to be made for sale must comply with the company's Angel Policy. Please contact your nearest demonstrator for more details.

Fifty Shades of Rubber Stamping - By Amanda Bartlett

Introduction

I have written this book to share with you some of my favourite techniques and to show you the wide range of things to do with rubber stamps. It is a wonderful hobby to have and lets you create beautiful and fun projects without having to be 'arty'. I have put together some projects to inspire you and to enjoy making. New techniques are being discovered all the time, so don't be afraid to experiment with the stamps. There are projects for both beginners and more experienced stampers, so there is something for everyone. I have indicated at the top of each project if it is suitable for a beginner or a more experienced stamper and have chosen many different techniques that can easily be adapted to use with all sorts of stamps.

The book contains fifty different ways of rubber stamping, and designed to be used as a reference guide for different techniques, and each technique has a project with it. So, the book can be used to refer to a particular technique, as well as an ideas book for projects to make.

Rubber Stamps

First of all let's look at the stamps themselves. There two main sorts of stamps available: wood mounted and clear mount rubber stamps. There are also other types available, but I shall be concentrating on these two.

<u>What's the difference between wood mounted and clear mount rubber stamps?</u>

Wooden rubber stamps have a wood block with a picture of the stamp on it, and the rubber stamp is attached to the underneath. This is easy to hold and stamp with. The only problem you may encounter is how to do very exact precision stamping as you cannot see exactly where you are stamping, so lining things up can be tricky. This problem is solved by using a 'Stamp-a-ma-jig' which is made by Stampin' Up!, and is a tool designed to eliminate this problem. We look into this further in Chapter 8 when using Builder stamps.

Clear mount rubber stamps are just the actual rubber stamp itself, so they tend to be cheaper than the wooden ones (as you are not paying for the wood). However, they need to be placed on to an acrylic block before use. Many different sized acrylic blocks are available. The stamps take up less room to store as they are smaller. Beware that some clear stamps vary widely in quality. A good quality stamp should stamp perfectly. A poor quality stamp will warp or squash as you press it and you will get smudged or distorted images. Of course, with a large stamp you will need to make sure that you have an acrylic block large enough for it to fit on to for a perfect impression. Acrylic blocks on their own can be used to make backgrounds which you will see later in the book in Chapter 9. More experienced stampers may sometimes like to stamp using bleach; this is not recommended on some makes of clear stamps (and you must clean your stamps immediately after use if using on wood mounted stamps).

<u>How to make the perfect impression</u>

We can use, amongst other things, brush marker pens, many different types of ink pads, and paints to colour our stamps. We will look at all of these in more detail in further chapters.

Ink Pads

When buying an ink pad I suggest you always choose a 'raised ink pad'. This means that when you remove the lid the ink pad is raised up from its base. Then you can tap the pad on to the stamp (yes that way round!) to cover the stamp in ink. The stamp can be as small or as large as you like. If the pad is not raised you are restricted to using a stamp which will fit inside the pad. Some of the projects I have designed use very large stamps. Examples of how to use them begin in Chapter 2.

How to re-ink an ink pad

As your ink pad uses up its ink you will notice it is paler in the centre as that part gets used up first. Simply add a few drops of the corresponding ink on top of the pad and spread the ink over the pad using the side of a bone folder. Leave for a few minutes to soak in and then try stamping to see how dark the image is. If necessary add more drops. It is important not to over ink the pad otherwise it is difficult to stamp crisp images. Some more specialist types of ink pads, for example, white ink pads, have a much thicker ink so they will need re-inking more often and the ink takes longer to soak into the pad. Sometimes ink pads can start to dip in the middle with a lot of use, which can make impressions look pale even though the stamp has plenty of ink. If this happens then it is time to replace the ink pad.

How to store ink pads

As you start to use your ink pads it is best to store them upside down, so that the ink will be at the surface of the ink pad ready for when you want to use it. Some ink pads are specially designed so that when you close it, the pad is already stored upside down.

Brush Marker Pens

Brush marker pens are specially designed to use directly on to rubber stamps. Ordinary pens can be difficult to clean off and can damage your stamp. Stamps are not cheap, so it best to use the proper pens so your stamps will last for years and years. Brush marker pens are usually double ended. One end is usually thicker so that it is easy to brush the colour on the the stamps as if the pen is a paint brush. The narrower end is used to add finer detail. One of the benefits of using brush marker pens is that you can get more than one colour on to the stamp before you actually stamp it. They also work especially well on stamps that have lots of solid (filled-in) areas rather than just outlines. For examples on how to use the pens see Chapter 1.

Paints

Paints can be used on solid (filled-in) rubber stamps where there is a large surface area for the paint to stick to. Different paints can be used on different surfaces, for example, fabric paint on a T-shirt (so it is washable) or acrylic paint on a ribbon to go on a present. See Chapter 5 for some ideas. Always clean your stamps immediately after use in case the paint permanently stains your stamps.

How to clean your stamps

If you are going to use a white ink on a dirty stamp then obviously the white ink will not look crisp, so it is important to clean your stamps. It is best to clean them as soon after you have used them as possible. Water-based ink pads, paints and brush marker pens can be cleaned with water. Simply wet a paper towel and repeatedly stamp on it until your stamp becomes clean and then dry with a clean paper towel. Baby wipes are also often used but you need to take care with these as some can damage clear stamps over time. Specialist ink pads (for example StazOn ink) need a stronger cleaner, so you can buy special stamp cleaners to clean your stamps as the water just won't remove it properly. To use them rub them directly on to the stamp and rub with a cloth and you will be surprised just how much ink comes off. You can also buy special stamp cleaning items; for example, Stampin' Up! have a 'Stampin' Scrub' which has washable foam pads (one can be sprayed with a special cleaner to wipe your stamps on, and the other is to dry the stamps on).

The stamps

In these examples I have often used the same stamps but in different projects. This is to illustrate how versatile stamps are, and how they can be used in many different ways. Also, with a bit of imagination some stamps can be used for other subjects than for which they are designed. An example of this is the Christmas baubles card in Chapter 8 which has been created using mosaic stamps and accessories.

Lets get stamping! There are 50 projects to make.

You will need your craft basics of scissors, bone folder, scrap paper, craft mat, ruler, 3D foam pads, glue, pencil, trimmer, strong red tape for sticking on embellishments and ribbons, and double sided tape. All other items needed are listed with each project. I have also used a heat gun, a Sizzex embossing and die cutting machine, and punches in many of my projects.

Chapter 1   Brush marker pens

When using brush marker pens directly on to a stamp you always start with the lightest colour first so you do not contaminate your pens. Many pens are double ended, with a wide end used to paint the colour on to the stamp, and the fine tip end used to add fine detail. Use the wide end of the pen to 'brush' on the ink. Then brush on the next lightest colour and finish with the darkest colour. If you are using a large stamp it may be that the ink may appear to be dry by the time you are ready to stamp. So breath on to the stamp (yes really! This is called 'huffing'). The moisture from your breath will be enough to dampen the ink so that you can stamp. When stamping press the stamp firmly on to the card but do not rock it or you may get unwanted marks, and then carefully lift up the stamp. You may be able to huff again and get another print or two.

Brush marker pens to create a water-colour effect   **Gift tags**
Beginner

Figure 1   Figure 2

The two gift tags at the top of Figure 1 are not spritzed with water and the two gift tags beneath them are, to illustrate the difference that spritzing makes. The spritzed gift tags look as if they are painted with watercolours by making the ink run.

You will need (see Figure 2):
A flower stamp (I used the Best of Flowers Stamp Set from Stampin' Up!)
Brush marker pens in different colours, and a fancy tag punch
White and pink card
A single hand held hole punch, and ribbon
Corner punch (optional), and a water spritzer

How to make them (see Figure 1):

Top left hand gift tag (not spritzed)
Use brush marker pens to colour directly on to the stamp. Use the wide tip of the brush marker pen and start with the palest colour, and finish with the darkest colour. 'Huff' on to the stamp and then stamp on to some white card. Punch out the stamped flowers using the fancy tag punch. Mount on to some pink card, and then on to some white card.

Cut some white card 6 cm x 10 cm and curve the corners with the corner punch. Measure half way (3 cm) along one of the short sides and make a pencil mark approximately 1 cm into the card to make a mark for the hole (not too close to the edge). Use the single hand held punch to make the hole and thread through some pink ribbon. Pad the flowers on to the tag.

Bottom left hand gift tag (spritzed)
Use brush marker pens to colour directly on to the stamp as described above. Use the spritzer to spray water on to the stamp. The stamp wants to be wet but not saturated. Stamp on to some spare white card. As the pen dries your image should look as if it is a water colour image. Punch out the stamped flowers using the fancy tag punch. Mount on to some pink card, and then on to some white card. Make the gift tag itself as described for the previous tag.

Top right hand gift tag (not spritzed)
Cut some white card to 10 cm x 6 cm. Use brush marker pens to colour directly on to the stamp. 'Huff' on to the stamp and then stamp on to the white card. 'Huff' again and stamp again. You will get a few impressions before the stamp runs out of colour. The first image will be the brightest so it needs to be at the bottom of the tag. As the colour fades each time you stamp, move it further up the card over-stamping previous images, so that the images are very pale by the time you reach the top of the card. You will need to re-colour the stamp and do this again to cover all of the tag in flowers. The brightest flowers at the bottom will look as if they are at the front, and the palest will look as if they are behind them giving a sense of perspective. Make a hole and add a ribbon as described above.

Bottom right hand gift tag (spritzed)
Cut some white card 10 cm x 6 cm. Use the wide tip end of the brush marker pens to colour directly on to the stamp, starting with the palest colour and working through to the darkest colour. Use the spritzer to spray water on to the stamp so it is wet but not saturated. Stamp on to the white card. Repeat until your stamp runs out of colour. Have the brightest images at the bottom of the tag and the palest near the top as for tag described above. You will need to re-colour the stamp and repeat also as described above. As the pen dries your image should look as if it is a water colour image. Make a hole and add a ribbon the same way as for the previous tags.

Suggestion: why not stamp on white paper to make some gift wrap using a matching colour ink?

***

You will need (see Figure 4):
Wildflower Meadow stamp from Stampin' Up! (or similar 'filled in' stamp)
Brush marker pens in different colours
Large scalloped circle punch (or similar)
Black ink pad, and some pink ribbon
Pre-folded white card 5" x 7"
White, pink and black card
Butterfly embosslits die or small butterfly punch
Greetings stamp with matching punches

How to make it (see Figure 3):
Ink up the Wildflower Meadow stamp in black ink and stamp on to some spare white card. Trim down to size around the image and mount on to some black card. Clean the stamp.

This time use the pens directly on to the stamp. Use the wide tip of the pen starting with the palest colour first, working through to the darkest. When you have finished applying the colour 'huff' and stamp on to some spare white card. Choose part of the stamped image which is very colourful and punch out with the large scalloped punch. Put 3D foam pads on the back of the scallop circle, line up the coloured image with the black image and stick on top. I like the contrast between the black background and the bright colours within the scallop circle.

Tie a pink ribbon around the card and tie in a knot or a bow. Stick on the stamped image. Die cut or punch out some butterflies in pink card and glue on to the card.

Stamp and punch out a greeting, stick on to a black mount and secure at the bottom of the card. I had plenty of coloured flowers left on my spare white card so I made a gift tag to match.

Why not try: this design but instead of using coloured pens, use embossed gold (or another colour) in your raised circle? For instructions on how to heat emboss see Chapter 6.

***

Brush marker pens and aqua-painters   **Father's Day card**
Beginner

Figure 5   Figure 6

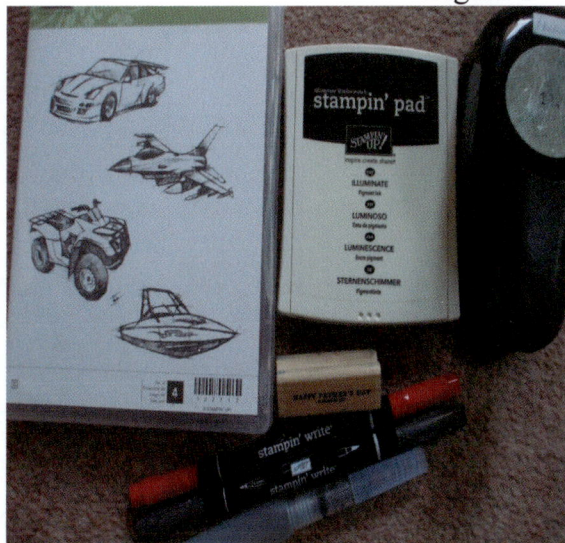

You will need (see Figure 6):
Need for Speed stamp set by Stampin' Up! (or similar)
Circle punch one and three quarters of an inch
Black A5 card folded in half and the corners curved with a corner punch
White, grey, red and black card
Brush marker pens in black and red
Illuminate ink pad, and an aqua-painter with water inside
Father's Day stamp and matching punches for mounts

How to make it (see Figure 5):
Use the wide tip end of the red brush marker pen to colour on to the car stamp (always start with the lightest colour first to avoid contamination). Then brush on black pen for the tyres. 'Huff' on to the stamp and then stamp on to some white card. You should have a red outline car with black tyres. Clean the stamp.

The ink in the pens is non-permanent which means that if we wet the ink it will bleed. Use the aqua-painter to carefully drag the red ink from the outline of the impression to colour in the car. Take care not to go over the outside lines, or to colour in the windows. Leave to dry, and then cut out leaving a small white edge all the way around the stamp.

Punch out a circle in red, white and black card. Position them so they are slightly overlapping and strap them together with a couple of pieces of tape. Then you can pick them up as one element, turn them over and stick them on to the grey card. Trim around the grey card, and mount on white card and trim again.

Position the pre-folded black card landscape. Ink up the stamp in the Illuminate ink pad and carefully stamp at the bottom left hand corner of the card. Line up the bottom of the stamp with the bottom and left hand side of the card so the stamp is straight. Re-ink the stamp and repeat for the bottom right hand side. Allow the ink to dry.

Stick on the mounted circles in the centre of the card and tape on the car. Use the brush marker pens to colour directly on to the greetings stamp to get the words in different colours. 'Huff' and stamp on to spare white card and punch out. Punch out a red mount and stick together at the top right hand corner of the card.

Why not try: this technique with a stamp where you use several different coloured marker pens?

***

White stamped image on black card and brush marker pens on top   Feathers card
Some experience

You will need (see Figure 8):
Fine Feathers stamp set from Stampin' Up!
White and black ink pads
Greetings stamp and matching punch
Black and coloured brush marker pens
Corner punch (optional), and some turquoise ribbon
Pre-folded 5" x 7" turquoise card, plus card in black, white and turquoise

How to make it (see Figure 7):
Use the corner punch to curve the corners of your pre-folded turquoise card. Ink up the smallest feather in the stamp set in black ink and randomly stamp all around the outside edge of the front of the card. Vary the direction of the stamp, re-inking each time you use it to get a consistent level of colour each time you stamp. Take the images off the edge of the card each time you stamp.

Figure 7   Figure 8

On spare black card stamp each of the remaining feathers in white ink across the bottom of the card. Leave to dry. Then trim down to 9.5 cm x 10.5 cm. If you have any extra white ink marks that you want to hide you can carefully colour over them with the black brush marker pen. It may take a couple of coats to completely cover the marks.

Use your brush marker pens to colour on top of the feathers. Bright and light colours show up the most. I also like to leave parts of the white ink untouched to show through as well. You can use more than one colour on each feather. As the pens dry the colouring is quite subtle. When you have finished colouring mount on to turquoise card, and then on to white card.

Cut a strip of white card to the same width as your mount, and tape some turquoise ribbon along it. Bring the ends of the ribbon to the back of the card and tape down to keep the front looking neat. Tie a separate knot in some more ribbon and tape it on to the centre of the ribbon taped on the card.

With black ink stamp a greeting and a couple of different feathers on spare white card. Punch out the greeting and cut out the feathers leaving a small white edge around them. Arrange the mounted feathers and the mounted ribbon on to some 11 cm x 15 cm black card and stick down. Then stick the whole thing on to the turquoise card. Glue on a feather on the left hand edge of the ribbon and then pad the second feather so it slightly overlaps it. Pad the greeting in the top right hand corner.

***

Chapter 2 Different coloured ink pads

There are so many different coloured ink pads available now, we don't have to stick to just a few primary colours. We can have ink pads that match our card stock, which match accessories like ribbon, so our projects can be colour co-ordinated. Most coloured ink pads are non-permanent, but some are permanent so you need to check this when you buy them depending on what you are going to make. I have used non-permanent ink pads for this chapter.

Stamping with different coloured ink pads   **3D Christmas presents card**
Some experience

Figure 9   Figure 10

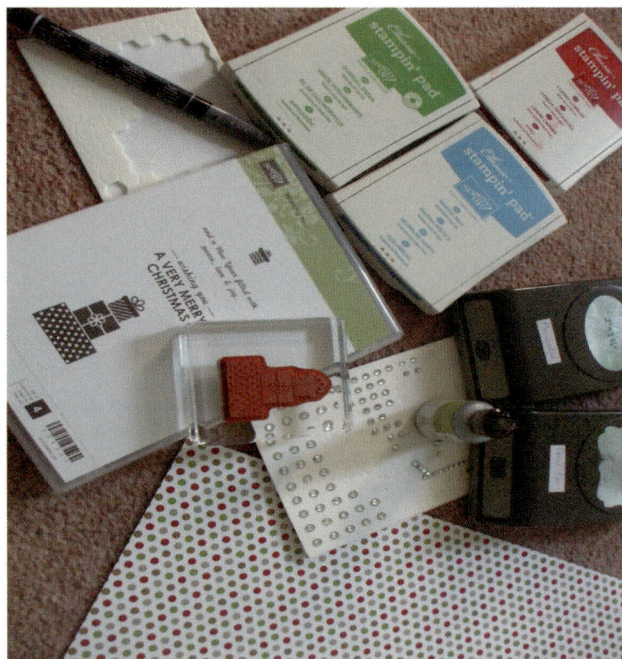

As you can see, the presents stamp I have used is quite small. So this example illustrates how you can use a repeat stamping technique to create a much larger image.

You will need (see Figure 10):
White DL card
Spare white and red card
Ink pads in green, red and blue
Fine tip black pen, and patterned paper
Silver glitter glue, and self adhesive gem stones
Presents stamp (I used the 'Wishing You' set from Stampin' Up!)
Large oval punch, and a decorative label punch

How to make the card (see Figure 9):
Open out your white DL card and cut off 3 cm from the right hand side of the *front* of the card only.

Ink up the presents stamp in red ink and stamp on spare white card, re-ink and stamp a second image. Clean the stamp and repeat in green ink and then blue ink.

Cut out all of the sections of the presents for one of the red stamped images and cut off the bow at the top. Repeat for one of the blue, and one of the green stamped images.

On some spare white card arrange on the presents. Leave a small space between each present. Working from top to bottom I have gone small green, medium red, large blue, small red, medium blue, large green, small blue, medium green and large red. Glue them down.

Use a fine tip black pen to draw carefully around each present. Make sure each black line is part of the next present. Draw a small bow on the top (the same as how it appears on the stamp).

Use your spare stamped images to cut out a small green present and pad it on top of the first identical present. Cut out a medium blue present and pad on top of the identical blue present. Then cut out the large red present and pad on top of the identical red present to 3D some of the presents.

Trim down the white card to 5 cm x 15 cm and mount on to red card. Trim this to size and stick on the front of your card leaving a large margin at the bottom for the greeting.

Stamp the greeting from the same stamp set in red ink and punched out with the oval punch. Punch out a red decorative label and pad the greeting on top. Tape the whole thing on to the bottom of the card.

Use gem stones to decorate the centres of the medium-sized presents and silver glitter glue to dot some sparkle on to the large presents.

Trim some patterned paper to 19.5 cm x 2.5 cm and tape on to a red mount. Trim to size and stick on the right-hand side of the inside of the card so that you can see it when the card is closed.

Suggestion: why not use the stamp to create a birthday or wedding version?

***

Stamping-off   **Bottle tag**
Beginner

You will need (see Figure 12):
Red and dark green ink pads
White card 6.5 cm x 13.5 cm with the corners curved with a corner punch
Scoring tool, and red ribbon
Circle punch one and three eighths of an inch, and a ruler
En Français stamp (from Stampin' Up!)
Swirls stamp and flowers stamps (I used the Everything Eleanor stamp set from Stampin' Up!)

Figure 11   Figure 12

How to make it (see Figure 11):

Position the white card portrait and place on some scrap paper. Ink up the En Français stamp in red ink and stamp on to some scrap paper, then stamp on to the white card. I have stamped mine deliberately at an angle rather than trying to line the stamp up straight. By stamping on to the scrap paper first it removes some of the ink so that when you stamp again the impression will be fainter. This makes a gentle background on the white card. This is called stamping-off.

Ink up the swirls in red ink and stamp on the white card, going over the top of the text. The impression clearly stands out against the paler background even though the same ink pad has been used.

We are going to use the same stamping off technique with the green flowers. Ink up a flower stamp in dark green and stamp on to some scrap paper. Then stamp it on to the stamped card taking the impression off the side of the card. Repeat in different places around the card. Ink up another flower in the green ink and stamp directly on to the card. Stamp in different places around the card, again taking some of the flowers off the side of the card and going over the top of the paler flowers.

Insert the top end of the bottle tag into the circle punch. Make sure the card is in as far as it goes and is evenly spaced on the left and right hand sides. Punch out a hole.

From the top of the card measure down 6.5 cm on the left and right hand sides and make pencil marks. Place a ruler between the pencil marks and score across the card. Finish off by tying some red ribbon through the circle and round the side of the bottle tag.

This makes an alternative way of presenting a bottle as a gift instead of in a bottle bag.

***

Use the same coloured ink as the card for a subtle impression   **Baby bib card**
Beginner   (Versamark ink pads can make a similar effect)

Figure 13   Figure 14

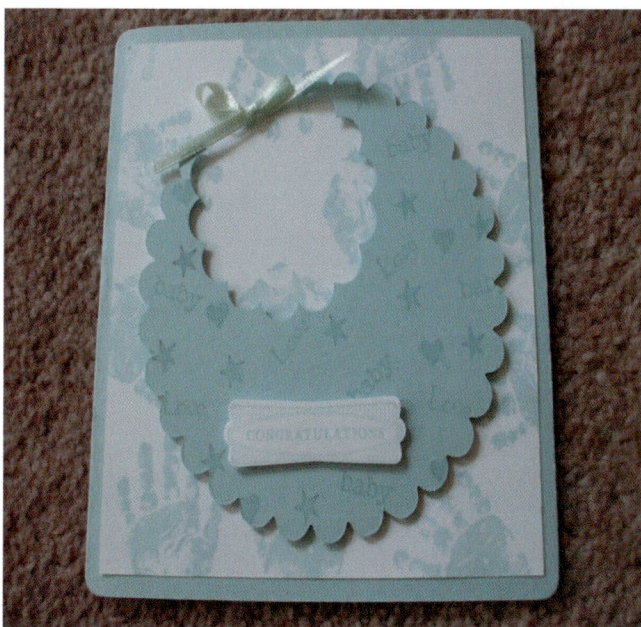

You will need (see Figure 14):
Large circle scallop die, and die cutting machine
Narrow blue ribbon, and some white card
Blue card and ink pad to match (I have used 'Soft Sky' from Stampin' Up!)
Large scallop circle punch (or plain circle punch)
Congratulations stamp, and matching punch
Square blue pre-folded card 144 mm, with the corners curved with a corner punch
Pennant Parade stamp set from Stampin' Up! (or similar small stamps)
Baby Prints stamp set from Stampin' Up!

How to make it (see Figure 13):
Cut some white card to 13 cm square. Place it on some scrap paper. Ink up the baby hand prints stamp in the blue ink and stamp around the outside of the card, taking the stamp off the edge of the card, varying direction and re-inking each time you stamp. Tape it on to the centre of the blue square pre-folded card.

Die cut a large scallop circle in blue card. Use the large scallop circle punch (or plain circle punch) to punch out of the side of the large scallop circle to make a bib shape.

Place the bib on some scrap paper and select some small stamps from the Pennant Parade stamp set. I have used 'baby', a star, 'love' and a heart stamps. Ink up one of the stamps in the blue ink and stamp over the bib, taking some off the edge of the card, leaving space for other stamps. The blue ink on the blue card gives a subtle impression. Repeat using the rest of the stamps. Take care not to stamp over the top of each other and try to keep them evenly spaced. The same effect can be achieved by using a Versamark ink pad and leaving it to dry to give a watermark type effect.

Pad the bib on to the card at a slight angle. Tie a bow and use a glue dot to hold it in place at the top of the bib. Stamp a blue greeting on white card and punch out. Pad at the bottom of the bib.

***

Over-stamping in different colours   **Bird house card**
Some experience

Figure 15   Figure 16

Figure 17

You will need (see Figures 16 and 17):
Card in brown, pale green, pale blue and beige
Small gem stones, and bakers twine
Bird punch, and heart punch
Greetings stamp with matching punches
Ink pads in pale pink, pale green, pale blue and brown
Everything Eleanor stamp set (from Stampin' Up!)
Corner punch, and a hand held single hole punch

How to make the card (see Figure 15):
Cut your brown card to A5 and fold in half. Curve the corners with a corner punch (optional).

Cut a piece of beige card to 9.5 cm x 13.5 cm, place on top of some scrap paper and position portrait.

Ink up the swirls stamp in the green ink and stamp on top of the beige card. Make sure the impression goes off the edge of the card. Re-ink the stamp each time you use it to make a consistent shade of green ink. I used the stamp coming in from all four corners of the card. It does not matter if you over-stamp on top of previous impressions (see Figure 17).

Ink up the largest flower stamp in pink. Stamp over the top of the green swirls. I concentrated the flowers near the top and bottom of the card. Again take the impressions off the sides of the card. You can make a few impressions before re-inking the stamp if you want some paler images (they will disappear into the background).

Repeat with the blue on the medium sized flower, this time concentrating across the mid section of the card. You should now have a busy and interesting background for your card. Tape this on to your brown card.

To make the birds, use the bird punch to punch out a bird and wing in green and blue card. Pad the green wing to the blue bird and vice versa. One bird faces left and the other faces right. Punch out the branch in brown card to use later on.

To make the bird house, on spare beige card punch out a heart. Discard the heart so you are left with the aperture. Trim the card on the left and right hand sides close to the heart. Trim the card along the bottom close to the heart. Now for the top of the bird house – measure 3 cm up from the central point of the heart and make a pencil mark. Place a ruler horizontally across the bird house but slightly up from the heart, and make pencils marks on the left and right hand sides. Pencil a line from the central dot diagonally downwards towards the pencil mark on the left and cut along this line to make the left hand slope for the roof. Repeat for the right hand side.

Ink up the swirls stamp again, this time in brown ink. Place your bird house on scrap paper and stamp the swirls on to the bird house. Stick the bird house on to some spare brown card and cut around it to make a mount.

Punch a small hole with a single hand held hole punch near the top point of the bird house (not too close to the edge!). Thread through some bakers twine and tie a bow but leaving a gap. Thread the bird house on to the brown branch so that it hangs. Glue the branch on to the top right hand side of the card.

Place sticky pads underneath the bird house to hold it in place. Glue a bird 'inside' the house.

Pad the second bird above the house, slightly overlapping the roof so it looks as if it is sitting on the roof.

Stamp a greeting in brown ink and punch out. Punch out a mount in brown card. Stick your greeting on to its mount and pad centrally at the bottom of the card.

***

Use colour ink pads with an aqua painter   **Retirement card**
Beginner

Figure 18

You will need (see Figure 19):
Terracotta DL card, plus some spare terracotta card
Cream card 20.5 cm x 9 cm
Watercolour card
An aqua-painter (with water in it)
Leaf stamp (I used the Lovely as a Tree stamp set by Stampin' Up!)
Single hand held hole punch and some narrow green ribbon
Patterned brown paper 19.5 cm x 6.5 cm, and a hand held single hole punch
Non-permanent ink pads in green, terracotta and dark brown
Greetings stamp and matching punches to mount

Figure 19

How to make it (see Figure 18):

Ink up the leaf stamp in terracotta ink and stamp on to the water colour card firmly (it can be textured so press it down well but don't rock the stamp). Use the aqua-painter to drag the colour around the outside edge of the image. Because the ink is non-permanent it will 'bleed' giving a nice colour shadow around the outside of the picture. Leave to dry and then trim down to 5.5 cm x 5 cm. Wipe the aqua-painter on to some scrap paper until the water runs clear. Repeat for the remaining two colours.

Mount the pictures on to terracotta card and trim down to size. Measure half way across the top of the picture and punch a hole (not too close to the edge) with the single hand held hole punch. Thread through some green ribbon, tie a knot and trim off the ends neatly.

Position the terracotta DL card landscape and tape on the cream card leaving an even margin all the way around. Tape on the patterned paper leaving an even margin at the top and sides, but a larger margin at the bottom (for the greeting).

Stick down the left and right hand tags so they are near the bottom of the card. Stick down the centre tag near the top of the card. Stamp a greeting in terracotta ink and punch out. Punch out a mount in terracotta card and stick together below the centre tag.

***

Figure 20   Figure 21

You will need (see Figure 21):
Green card 13 cm square, and some terracotta card
Pre-folded cream card 144 mm square, and some spare cream card
Watercolour card, and an aqua-painter (with water in it)
Leaf stamp (I used the Lovely as a Tree stamp set by Stampin' Up!)
Hessian ribbon, and a corner punch
Non-permanent ink pads in green, terracotta and dark brown
Greetings stamp and matching punch

How to make it (see Figure 20):
I have used the same stamps and colours as the previous card to illustrate the difference between the
two techniques, but using the same equipment.

Ink up the leaf stamp in terracotta ink and stamp on to the water colour card firmly (it can be textured
so press it down well but don't rock the stamp). Use the aqua-painter to paint over the image. Because
the ink is non-permanent it will 'bleed' thereby colouring in the image. I have deliberately not coloured
all of the image in as I like the spaces showing, this adds another dimension to the image. Also do not
over-work the painting otherwise you may lose some of the detail. Do not go over the outside lines.
Leave to dry and then trim down to 5.5 cm x 5 cm. Wipe the aqua-painter on to some scrap paper until
the water runs clear. Repeat for the remaining two colours. I used the tip of the aqua-painter in the
terracotta ink pad to paint in the shiny brown colour of the acorn for each of the images.

Ink up the leaf stamp in terracotta ink and stamp in the bottom right hand corner of the terracotta card.
Even though the pad is the same colour as the card you can still see the impression. Arrange the

painted leaves around it to make a block of four and stick down. Trim down leaving a small margin all the way around. Mount on to cream card and trim down leaving a small margin again.

Use a corner punch to curve the corners of the pre-folded cream card. Place the green square card at an angle so all of the corners go off the edges of the cream card and stick down. Turn over the cream card and cut off all the excess green card. Turn back over to face the front again.

Stick the mounted leaves in the centre of the card. Tie a knot (not too tight or it will be very bulky) and stick across the top of the card. I used red tape to attach this as it is very strong. Stamp a greeting on spare cream card and punch out with a tag punch. Mount it on to some terracotta card and trim down to size. Pad in place across the centre of the card.

***

Tiles   **Just for you blue and white card**
Beginner

Figure 22   Figure 23

You will need (see Figure 23):
A large stamp (I used the Wildflower Meadow stamp from Stampin' Up!)
Good quality white card larger than your stamp
5" x 7" white pre-folded card with the corners curved with a corner punch
Navy card to mount, and a navy ink pad
Scoring tool and scoring board (optional)
Greetings stamp and matching punches

How to make it (see Figure 22):
I have chosen to make this card in navy and white as it reminds me of the tiles in the Mediterranean.

I have made this card using a scoring board. If you do not have one you can do the measurements with a ruler. Place the good quality white card on to the scoring board. Use a fine ended scoring tool to score a line every 2 cms. Press firmly (this is why you need to use a good quality card so it does not tear). Turn your card around ninety degrees and repeat so you have lots of squares (do not turn the card over).

Place the scored card in front of you exactly as it was on the scoring board (do not turn the card over). Position it portrait. Ink up your stamp in navy ink and stamp on to the card. As this is a large stamp make sure you press firmly all over. Remove the stamp.

The ink should appear on the 'tiles' and be absent from the grooves that you scored, giving a tile effect to the picture. Trim down to size and mount on some navy card. Mount the whole thing on to the white pre-folded card. Stamp and punch out a greeting and mount and stick in the top left hand corner to finish off. I liked the simplicity of this card, but you can add more embellishments if you feel it needs it.

***

Make your own multicoloured ink pads   **Easter card**
Some experience

To make your own multicoloured ink pads you will need (see Figure 25):
Some different coloured ink refills (the type used to refill your ink pads), I used green, orange and yellow
Some felt (a light colour so the ink shows up on it)
An old piece of plastic to put the felt on (a plastic bag will do)
Flowers stamp (I used Serene Silhouettes from Stampin' Up!)
Happy Easter stamp, and matching punches
Yellow card for mounting, and some patterned paper 9 cm x 13.5 cm
White A5 card folded in half and the corners curved with a corner punch, and some spare white card

How to make a multi-coloured ink pad:
Place the felt on top of the plastic. Add a few drops of your first coloured ink on the left hand side. Add a few drops of your second coloured ink slightly further along the felt, and so on. I tend to go from light to dark so I have used yellow, orange then green. The ink soaks into the felt (and through it) so it is essential to have some plastic underneath.

Figure 24   Figure 25

How to make the card (see Figure 24):

Make your multi-coloured ink pad as described above. Tap your stamp on top of the ink pad several times to ensure the stamp is covered in ink. Keep the stamp in a similar place each time your tap it on to the felt. Although we want the whole stamp inked up, we do not want to mix up the colours on the stamp, so we can get a striped look by one colour turning into another colour. If we mix up too much we end up with another effect again.

Stamp the flower on to white card and then trim down to size. Mount on some yellow card.

Stamp a greeting on your felt ink pad and punch out. Punch out a yellow mount and stick together.

Tape the patterned paper on to the white folded card. Stick on the mounted flower in the centre, leaving a larger margin at the bottom, then tape on the greeting directly below.

***

Figure 26   Figure 27

You will need (see Figure 27):
Cream pre-folded 5" x 7" card, with the corners curved with a corner punch
Cream card 10.5 cm x 14 cm, plus some extra cream card
Red card, and red ribbon
Everything Eleanor stamp set by Stampin' Up!, and a heat gun
Gold mirri card, and low tack masking tape
Versamark ink pad, and gold embossing powder
Anti-static pad, and a finger dauber
Sahara Sand ink pad, and a large heart punch
En Français text background stamp from Stampin' Up!
Anniversary greetings stamp and matching punches
Circle punch, and gold peel off numbers

How to make it (see Figure 26):
Ink up the En Français text stamp in the Sahara Sand ink pad and stamp on the cream 10.5 cm x 14 cm card. It doesn't have to be straight and the stamp is bigger than the card so it will go off the sides. Let the ink dry thoroughly.

Wipe over the text with an anti-static pad. Ink up the swirls stamp in the Versamark ink pad and stamp over the text, taking it off the sides of the card. Re-ink and do a second impression further down (it doesn't matter if the impressions overlap). Sprinkle on gold embossing powder, tap away the excess powder and heat fix with a heat gun (using a heat gun is covered in more detail in Chapter 6). Mount on to gold mirri card and trim to size.

Punch out a heart out of spare cream card, not too near the edge to make a stencil. Place the stencil over the text, and keep in place with some low tack masking tape. Ink up a flowers stamp in red ink and stamp over the stencil. Part of the flower will appear inside the stencil, but will not make a definite heart shape. Daub red ink inside the stencil with a finger dauber and a definite heart shape will appear.

Use the heart shape you punched out to decorate the second heart. Stamp over the top of the heart with the flower stamp and daub over it with red ink using a finger dauber. Pad the heart slightly below the first one.

Cut two pieces of ribbon. Tape one end of ribbon to the back of the card near the bottom and bring the ribbon round to the front. Do the same with the second piece on the other side. Tie a bow at the front of the card. Mount the whole thing on to red card. Then stick it on to the pre-folded cream card leaving a slightly larger margin at the bottom of the card for the greeting.

Stamp a greeting in red ink on cream card and punch out. Stick on to a red mount and pad in the centre of the bottom of the card. If it is a special anniversary punch out a red circle and pad on the top right hand corner of the card and use gold peel off numbers to finish off.

***

Repeat stamping for 'moving' images   **Motorbike card**
Beginner

You will need (see Figure 29):
Silver glitter glue
White A5 card, and some spare white card
Black and white striped Washi tape
Black card, and a black ink pad
Rev Up the Fun stamp set by Stampin' Up!

How to make it (see Figure 28):
Ink up the motorbike stamp in black ink. Position some spare white card landscape so you have plenty of space to move across the card. As our motorbike is facing towards the right hand side on the stamp, we will start stamping at the right hand side of the card and work towards the left. Line up the stamp with the bottom of the card and stamp your first impression at the right hand side. 'Huff' on the stamp (do not re-ink it) and move it left, line up the right hand side of the stamp with the edge of the front wheel and the bottom of the stamp in line with the card, and stamp again. Move along the stamp again with the edge of the front wheel and the bottom of the stamp lined up, and so on until you run out of ink. The whole process needs to be done precisely but quite quickly so that the ink doesn't dry. This is a fun technique that works well with any image depicting movement.

Figure 28   Figure 29

Trim down the stamped card to 14 cm x 5 cm, and mount on to some black card. Put some glitter glue on the logo on the motorbike. I also put some across the 'ground'. I had it thicker underneath the wheels of the first bike, and then it fades into nothing as it goes further towards the left hand side. Leave to dry, then mount on to some black card and trim down to size.

Fold the A5 white card in half and position landscape. Stick on some black and white striped Washi tape just inside the top and bottom of the card. Stamp up a greeting on some spare white card, trim to size and mount on to some black card.

Stick on the stamped section just above the bottom Washi tape. Tape on the greeting just below the top Washi tape in the middle, so that it overlaps the stamped section.

***

Using coloured ink pads with a blender pen   **Wedding card**
Beginner

You will need (see Figure 31):
Blender pen
White pre-folded card 5" x 7" with the corners curved with a corner punch
White card, and pale pink card
Bright pink ink pad
Self-adhesive lace tape
Self-adhesive pearls
A heart punch
Everything Eleanor stamp set by Stampin' Up!
Greetings stamp and matching punch

Figure 30   Figure 31

How to make it (see Figure 30):

Cut the lace tape into a section of 5 flowers, 4 flowers and 3 flowers. Stick the tape on to strips of pink card and trim down to size.

Cut some white card to 11 cm x 13.5 cm and position portrait. Ink up the swirls stamp in pink ink and stamp in each corner of the card, re-inking each time you stamp to keep the impressions bright. Take the impressions off the sides of the card. Mount on to pale pink card and trim to size. Tape on to the pre-folded white card leaving a much larger margin at the bottom for the greeting.

On spare white card stamp the smallest flower from the Everything Eleanor stamp set nine times, re-inking each time you stamp it. Use the blender pen to colour in the flowers. Do this by dipping the tip of the pen into the pink ink pad and then colouring on the flower. As you start colouring the pink will be bright, and as the colour runs out it will become paler. The colour will be paler than the outline of the stamp, so we will see all the detail of the stamp even though we are colouring in using the same ink pad. Cut out the flowers as close to the edges as possible.

Ink up the tag stamp in pink ink and stamp on spare white card. Do this again to make two separate images. Cut out one image leaving a small white gap all around the outside edge. Stamp a greeting on spare white card, punch out and tape in the centre of the pink tag. Punch out a heart shape through the second tag. This stamp is deliberately designed to look distressed, so it will not make a perfectly clear impression.

Tape the heart to the back of the smallest tier of the cake so that it sticks up in the middle. Arrange the tiers on the decorated white card leaving a gap between the tiers for the flowers. Stick down the tiers. Arrange on the flowers so they slightly overlap each other so that there are no gaps (4 in the top gap and 5 in the lower gap). Glue down in place.

Stick on the mounted greeting at the bottom of the card in the centre so that it partly overlaps the bottom tier of the cake. Finish with small self-adhesive pearls in the centre of each of the white lace flowers.

Why not try: these pens are very versatile. Why not try with chalks, or use more than one colour from your ink pads, so as one colour starts to pale it can blend into another colour?

***

Using an Illuminate ink pad
Some experience

Black and cream Wildflower Meadow card

Figure 32

Figure 33

Illuminate ink works well on different shades of card. When the light catches the ink it has a lovely shine to it. I really like it on black card. It takes longer than most other ink pads to dry.

You will need (see Figure 33):
A pre-scored 5" x 7" cream card
Patterned paper in black and cream 11.5 cm x 16.5 cm
Narrow black ribbon
Wildflower Meadow stamp and embossing folder (from Stampin' Up!)
Silver glitter glue
Silver mirri card, and some black card
Greeting stamp, and an Illuminate ink pad
Embossing machine

How to make it (see Figure 32):
Ink up the Wildflower Meadow stamp in Illuminate ink and stamp on to some black card. Leave to dry.

Insert the stamped image face up in to the matching embossing folder taking care to line up the images, and emboss through the embossing machine.

Slice the image into 3 cm width lengths of card. Mount these on to silver mirri card. Stick these on to the patterned paper with equal distances between the panels. Mount this on to black card, then stick the whole thing on to your pre-folded cream card.

Stamp a greeting on spare black card in Illuminate ink. I used 'smile'. Trim down to size and mount on silver mirri card. Pad at the centre of the bottom of the card.

Tie a bow in narrow black ribbon and glue in the top left hand corner. Finish off by using silver glitter glue in the centre of the flowers and in the eye of the bird.

Why not try: using the Illuminate ink pad on white card for a subtle background, or on different coloured card stock?

***

Only using small parts of the stamp(s)   **Cars and bikes card**
Beginner

Figure 34   Figure 35

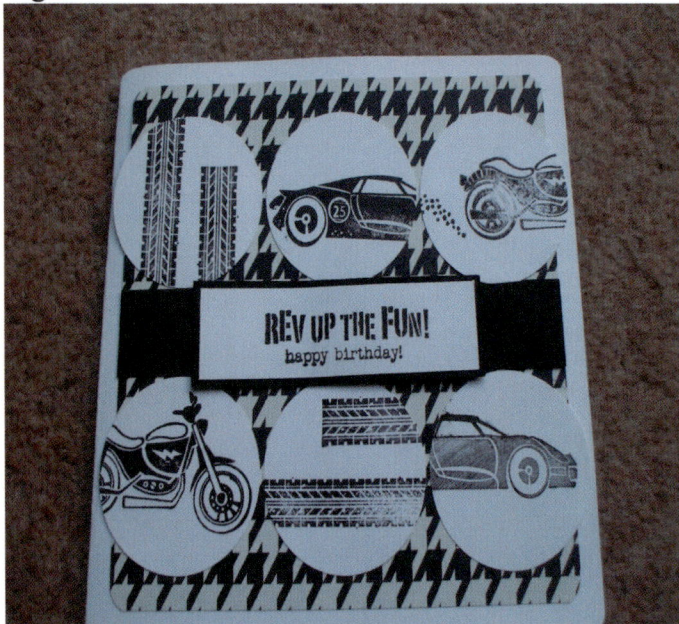

You will need (see Figure 35):
Rubber stamps with cars and bikes (I used 'Rev Up the Fun!' stamp set from Stampin' Up!)
Black ink pad, and spare black card
Black and white patterned paper 12.5 cm squared
Square white 14 cm pre-folded card
Spare white card

Black card 12.5 cm x 2 cm
Spare black card, and a corner punch
One and three quarters of an inch circle punch

How to make it (see Figure 34):
Use the corner punch to curve the corners on both the patterned paper and the pre-folded white card. Stick the patterned paper on to the centre of the white card. Tape on the black strip of card going across the centre of the card horizontally.

On spare white card use the black ink pad to stamp the car and motorbike twice, re-inking the stamps each time you use them to make sure you have very dark impressions. Then stamp the tyre marks starting in different places but keeping an equal distance between them so they are parallel. Also do this twice so you have six different stamped images.

Each image will not fit inside the circle punch so we only punch out part of the images. For each image that is duplicated punch out in a different place from last time. For example I have a circle with the front of the car, and a circle with the back of the car. I did the same for the motorbike.

Arrange the circles on the card, three at the top and three at the bottom. I turned the circles with the tyre marks to face different directions. The circles will slightly overlap the patterned paper.

Stamp the greeting in black ink on spare white card and trim down to size. Stick on to some spare black card and trim down as a mount. Pad on to the centre of the black strip in the middle of the card.

Why not try: this technique but stamping each image in a different colour for another effect? Or alternatively use one large stamp but punch out different sections of it.

***

Stamping on patterned paper   **Yellow/black birthday card**
Beginner

You will need (see Figure 37):
Patterned paper not too dark (I used yellow/white)
Yellow card for mounting, and spare white card
White pre-folded 144 mm square card, and a black ink pad
Wide white ribbon, and yellow liquid pearls
Large flower stamp (I used Sweet Floral from Stampin' Up!)
Greetings stamp with matching punches

To make the card (see Figure 36):
Ink up your large stamp in black ink. Make sure it is completely covered in ink. Stamp on to the patterned paper. Press firmly all over the stamp without rocking. When using a large stamp it can be easy to miss part of the stamp so make sure you press all of it. Carefully remove the stamp.

Figure 36   Figure 37

Trim down the stamped image to 13 cm square. It doesn't matter if you trim off part of the image. Mount this on to the yellow card and trim to size.

Turn over the yellow card and put some double sided tape across the bottom of the card coming up approx 2 cms from the bottom. Cut a length of white ribbon and lay across the tape so you have plenty of ribbon at either side. Put double sided tape on the remaining sides and turn over. Tape it on to the front of the white square folded card so that the ribbon ends are now brought to the front and tie a bow. Trim the ribbon ends at an angle so they don't fray.

Stamp a greeting in black ink and punch out. Punch out a yellow mount and stick together. Pad on to the top left hand corner of the card. Finish off by adding yellow liquid pearls in the centre of the flowers.

This technique works best with a light coloured patterned paper so the black ink stands out against it.

Why not try: this idea but using a dark patterned paper with an image stamped in white ink which also makes a good contrast?

***

Figure 38

Figure 39

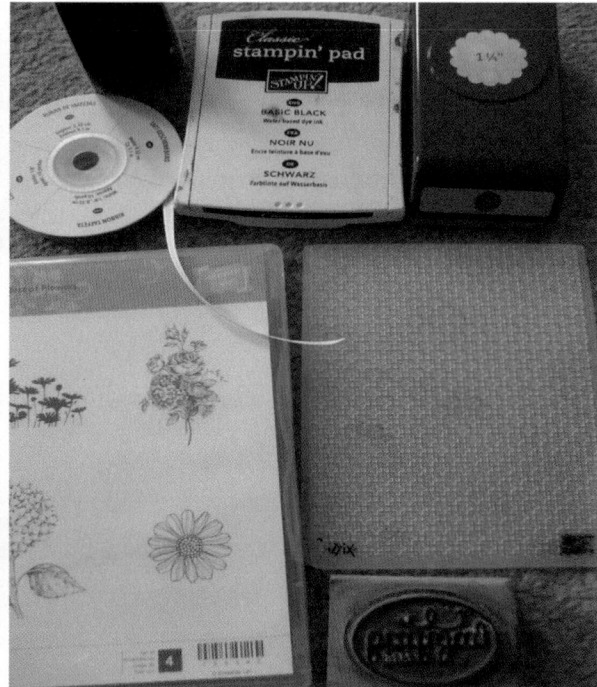

You will need (see Figure 39):
Cream 5" x 7" pre-folded card with the corners curved with a corner punch
Spare cream card, and some self-adhesive pearls
Daisy stamp (I used Best of Flowers Stamp set from Stampin' Up!)
Black ink pad, and black card
Black sheer ribbon, and narrow cream ribbon
Happy Birthday stamp, and oval punch
One and a quarter of an inch scalloped circle punch
Basket weave embossing folder, and embossing machine

How to make it (see Figure 38):
Cut some cream card to 10.5 cm x 13.5 cm. Ink up the daisy in black ink and randomly stamp on to the card, taking some of the impressions off the side of the card. Re-ink each time you stamp so you get consistent dark impressions. Do not stamp the images over the top of each other, and try to space them fairly evenly. Place the stamped card inside the basket weave embossing folder face up, and emboss through an embossing machine.

Mount on to some black card and trim to size. Cut two pieces of black ribbon and tape one end to the back of one side approx 2 cms up from the bottom. Stick the second piece of black ribbon to the back of the the other side and bring both ribbon ends to the front of the card and tie a bow towards the right hand side.

Tape the whole thing on to the pre-folded cream card leaving a larger margin at the bottom. Stamp and punch a greeting and stick towards the left hand side at the bottom of the card overlapping the textured card. Thread some cream narrow ribbon underneath the black bow and tie another bow on the top.

Stamp 3 daises on spare cream card and punch out with the scallop punch. Pad on to the top of the card. Finish off with self-adhesive pearls in the centres of the raised flowers, and a line of 3 pearls across the bottom right hand corner.

***

Masking objects   **Phone box card**
Some experience

Figure 40   Figure 41

You will need (Figure 41):
Black ink pad, and red pen to colour in
Tree stamp (Lovely as a Tree stamp set from Stampin' Up!)
Fine dazzling diamonds glitter, and fine tip glue pen
Telephone box or post box stamp, and a greetings stamp (I used Stampin Up! stamps)
A5 white card folded in half, and a large post-it-note
White card cut to 14 cm x 7 cm, and spare black card

How to make it (Figure 40):
Stamp the telephone box on to a post-it-note so that you will get some of the sticky part underneath your image. Cut out, this is your mask.

Position your rectangle of white card landscape. Ink up the phone box in the black ink and stamp towards the right hand side of the card. Do this carefully and press firmly but do not wobble so you get a nice crisp image. Place your mask directly on top of your stamped phone box.

Ink up the trees stamp in black ink. I used the stamp with several trees on it. Stamp the trees so that they come off the side of the card. Re-ink and stamp again moving across the card. You can over-stamp the trees to make them look more dense. As you go across the card to the right hand side stamp over the top of your mask carefully, and continue until the trees come off the right hand side of the card. When you stamp over the mask, make sure you press firmly as you can get a slight gap around the edge of the mask. When you are satisfied that you have plenty of trees you can remove the mask.

Mount on to black card, trim to size and stick on to the white pre-scored card positioned landscape. Leave a slightly larger margin at the bottom of the card for a greeting.

Colour in the phone box red (careful not to colour in the windows!). Leave the pen to dry. Use the glue pen and glitter to add some sparkle in the corners of the windows, on the trees and at the bottom of the trunks. Stamp and punch out a greeting and stick at the bottom of the card.

Tip: why not keep your masks together with your stamps so that next time you want to use a mask you will have one ready to use? The masks can be used over and over again.

***

Background masking
Some experience

Quad bike card

Figure 42

Figure 43

You will need (see Figure 43):
A red felt tip pen, and some scrap paper
Low tack masking tape
Pre-folded 5" x 7" brown card with the corners curved with a corner punch
A6 cream card, plus some spare cream card
White card 11 cm x 9 cm, and some spare brown card for a mount
Brown ink pad, and a finger dauber
Rev Up the Fun! Stamp set by Stampin' Up!
Need for Speed stamp set by Stampin' Up!

How to make it (see Figure 42):
Tear the scrap paper to make a rugged edge which we can use as a mask for the mud tracks.

Position the white card landscape. Position the torn paper so the torn edge faces downwards, about half way down the white card. Hold in place with low tack masking tape. Use a finger dauber to daub brown ink from the ink pad, starting on the scrap paper in downward motions, all the way along the torn edge. Remove the scrap paper and you should have your first mud track line.

Move the paper a bit further down the card, perhaps use a different part of the paper to vary the line of the track. Daub again, starting on the scrap paper and working in downward motions. Repeat until you reach the bottom. If there are any gaps in the mud tracks daub in some ink to fill them in.

Ink up the quad bike in dark brown ink and carefully position it so the tyres are in the mud but the rest of the bike is above it. Colour in the quad bike with red pen.

While you still have some brown ink on the finger dauber, daub in the top half of the white card to make that look dusty. Make sure the ink is not too dark when you do this, so if you need to reload your dauber with ink, take some off first on scrap paper so it is not so dark when you come to daub the dust.

Mount on to brown card and trim to size. Stamp a greeting in brown ink on some spare cream card and trim down to size. Stick on the bottom left hand corner of the picture.

Ink up the tyre track in brown ink, place your cream card landscape on some scrap paper, and stamp a tyre on the bottom left hand side very close to the side of the card, and ensuring that the impression goes off the bottom of the card. Do the same for the opposite corner (top right).

Mount the picture on to the cream card, and then mount the whole thing on to the dark brown pre-folded card.

***

Shadow stamping   **Note book**
Beginner

You will need:
A spiral bound note book
Pink card cut to fit on the front of your note book leaving a small edge all the way around
Black and white ink pads

Flower stamp (or similar stamp) I used Pocket Silhouettes from Stampin' Up!
Ribbons in pink, white and black

Figure 44

How to make it (see Figure 44):

The type of stamp you use is important. It needs to be something that you do not colour in (a filled-in stamp), but equally not too big a solid area either. So something like a snowflake, or simple flower designs work best. Try out different stamps on scrap paper first to see which stamps work best with this technique. It also works best on brightly coloured card so that the black and white inks really stand out.

Place your pink card on some scrap paper. Ink up the flower stamp in the black ink and start to stamp over the pink card. Re-ink the stamp each time you use it for even coverage. I have varied the direction of the stamp each time I have used it and tried to leave similar sized gaps between each stamp. Take the stamp off the edges of the card. Clean your stamp thoroughly when you have finished.

Now switch to the white ink pad and repeat. You are going over the top of all your stamped black images. As you stamp over the top you will want to miss slightly, in other words you are not going exactly over the top (something that would be very difficult to to do anyway). This creates the shadow effect with the black ink showing through the white. Leave to dry.

Tape the decorated pink card on to the front of your note book. I have finished off by tying scraps of ribbons in knots in matching colours around each of the spirals. I have done this randomly using different types of ribbons. Trim the ends quite short at an angle so they don't fray.

***

Stamping on glass   **Candle holder**
Beginner

Figure 45

You will need (see Figure 45):
A plain glass tumbler
Different coloured glass paints (I used yellow, red and blue)
A StazOn ink pad in black
A solid/filled in picture stamp (not an outline stamp), I used Pocket Silhouettes from Stampin' Up!
An old sponge cut into 3 (or as many colours as you are using)
Rubbing alcohol and paper towel

How to make it:
First clean the glass to remove any finger prints. Use some rubbing alcohol to clean it, and wipe it down with a paper towel. Leave for 10 minutes to dry.

Tip a small amount of yellow glass paint into an old saucer and use a piece of sponge to dab on paint around the base of the glass. You can put your hand inside the tumbler to help move it around. Repeat with the red colour moving further up the glass. Using a sponge gives an even layer of paint. Repeat again with the blue paint at the top of the glass. Do not paint the bottom of the glass. Leave the paint to dry for a couple of hours.

Ink up your stamp in black StazOn ink and slightly tip your glass on to its side. To stamp on to the glass we need to allow for the fact that the glass is curved. So press down one side of the stamp and then carefully 'roll' the stamp so that all of the stamp covers the surface of the glass. Carefully remove the stamp. Repeat to stamp the flowers all around the glass. Leave for 24 hours before you heat fix the paint.

To heat fix the paint follow the manufacturer's instructions on the bottles of glass paint. The glass needs to be placed on a lined baking tray into a cold oven so that it heats up gradually. This is to stop sudden heat from breaking the glass. Heat fixing the paint will make your item washable. Do not use in a dishwasher.

***

Stamping on a poly bag   **Halloween treats**
Beginner

Figure 46   Figure 47

You will need (see Figure 47):
Self sealing poly bag
StazOn ink pad
Halloween stamps, (I used Googly Ghouls from Stampin' Up!)
Googly eyes, and a stapler
Orange card
Some sweets

How to make it (see Figure 46):
Place the poly bag on to some white paper so that you can see your stamping more easily. Ink up a stamp in the StazOn ink and stamp on to the poly bag. We must use StazOn ink as a non-permanent ink will not dry on the plastic. Re-ink and continue to stamp on the bag using various Halloween stamps. Fill your bag with treats. Seal the bag closed.

Cut the orange card to the same width as your poly bag, and cut it twice the height as you would like it to look from the front. It will need to hide the self-sealing part of the poly bag. Fold the orange card in half so that it fits on top of the bag. Stamp some bats in black ink across the top of the card. Staple the orange card to the poly bag.

Stamp some Halloween images on spare white card, colour in and cut out. When cutting out leave a small white edge around the stamped image. Glue on to the orange card to hide the staples. Add googly eyes to finish off.

Why not try: there are many different uses for this idea. Why not stamp a poly bag with flowers and fill it with bath bombs as a little gift for friends, or perhaps decorate with celebration stamps to hand out at a birthday party?

***

Stamping on vellum   **Penguins card**
Some experience

Figure 48   Figure 49

You will need (see Figure 49):
Penguin stamp (I used Zoo Review by Stampin' Up!)
Black StazOn ink pad
Soft mat, and piercing tool

2 silver brads, and silver glitter glue
Blue/white bakers twine, and A5 vellum
Christmas greeting and matching punches
A5 white card, plus some spare white card
Approx 4 strips of card in different shades of blue and grey (all at least 15 cm long), widths can vary

How to make it (see Figure 48):
Cut a sliver off one of the short sides of the white A5 card (this is so that when we put the vellum sleeve on top, the white card is slightly shorter so it won't stick out at the bottom). Fold the white card in half and position landscape.

Tear along one of the long edges of each of the 4 strips of coloured card to get a rugged edge. Place one strip with the rugged edge at the top and the straight edge at the bottom. Take a second strip, position the same way, and put tape along the back of the strip (near the top). Tape this strip on to the first strip so you see both rugged edges. Repeat this for the rest of the strips so you end up with all four rugged edges showing and the pieces have become one element. This makes an interesting background to show through the vellum.

Place the torn piece so the straight edge is at the bottom of the pre-folded white card and the top torn edge should be about two thirds of the way up the card leaving white card showing at the top. Stick down in place and trim off the excess coloured card.

Fold the vellum in half and position landscape. Ink up a penguin in black StazOn ink (we must use a permanent ink when stamping on vellum otherwise the ink will not dry). Stamp the penguin near the left hand side about half way down. Re-ink and stamp another one beside it, and so on, working all the way across the vellum.

Stamp a greeting in black ink on spare white card and punch out. Punch out a mount in blue card and stick the two together. Open out the vellum and place a soft mat underneath. Position the greeting in the top left hand corner of the front of the vellum and pierce a hole through both the greeting and the vellum on the left hand side. Insert silver brads.

Slide the vellum sleeve over the white card. Hold them together with the bakers twine. Make sure it goes inside the white card and the vellum, then tie the ends together at the front in a tight knot or bow. If you lift up the vellum you can put some double sided tape underneath the greeting and tape it to the white card (as the tape is hidden under the greeting you will not see it through the vellum).

Finish off with sliver glitter glue dotted along the path of the penguins and just beneath them to show the sparkling ice.

***

Stamping on acetate   **Black and white Christmas trees card**
Some experience

You will need (see Figure 51):
White StazOn ink pad

Black ink pad, and some acetate
Evergreen stamp set by Stampin' Up!
Black and white sheer ribbons
Soft mat and piercing tool
Silver brads, and a frosted finishes embellishment (or similar)
Christmas greeting and matching punches
White pre-folded 5" x 7" card with the corners curved with a corner punch
White card 13 cm x 9 cm
Spare white and black card

Figure 50   Figure 51

How to make it (see Figure 50):
Place the 13 cm x 9 cm white card landscape and ink up the solid Christmas tree stamp in black ink. Stamp on the left hand side. Line the bottom of the stamp up with the bottom of the card so that the impression will be straight. It doesn't matter if the image goes slightly off the side of the card. Re-ink the stamp and do the same for the right hand side. Remember to line up the bottom of the stamp with the bottom of the card to keep it straight, and so that both trees will be in line. Stick on to black card and trim around to make a mount. Clean the stamp thoroughly.

Ink up the stamp again but this time in the white StazOn ink. We must use a permanent ink on acetate (non-permanent inks will not dry). Stamp on to the acetate. Leave to dry.

Cut a strip of black card 4.5 cm x 9 cm. Place portrait underneath the acetate. The white tree should stand out clearly on top of the black. Keeping them together place them on top of a soft mat. Use a piercing tool to poke a hole in each corner and brad the acetate and black card together. Once they are fixed together turn over the black card and trim off all the excess acetate. Use red tape to stick a decoration at the top of the tree.

Pad the white tree to the centre of the white card we decorated with black trees earlier on. Position the pre-folded white card landscape and stick the whole thing on to the white card leaving a slightly larger margin at the top of the card (for the bow and greeting). Cut a length of black and white ribbons. Holding the two together tie a bow so you have black and white loops and tails. Trim the ends neatly and use red tape to stick above the centre of the acetate tree.

Stamp a greeting in black ink on white card and punch out. Punch out a mount in black card and stick together. Tape the whole thing on to the top of the card above the bow.

***

Shrink plastic   **Black and white flowers card**
Some experience

Figure 52

To stamp on shrink plastic you must use a permanent ink – StazOn inks are ideal. Non-permanent inks will not dry. Stamp on to the matt side of the shrink plastic (check manufacturer's instructions). You also need large stamps, as the plastic when heated will shrink several times, and if any colour is added it will appear brighter. If you are making a key ring, beads or buttons, you need to punch the holes before the plastic is shrunk.

You will need (see Figure 52):
Black StazOn ink pad, and a white StazOn ink pad
Shrink plastic: black, white and cream
Rubber stamps with large designs: I used the clear Mixed Bunch stamp set from Stampin' Up!
Punch to go with stamps or scissors to cut out the images
Black card 4 cm x 9 cm, and some self adhesive pearls
Black and white polka-dot ribbon
White card 9 cm x 12.75 cm when folded in half
Heat gun (optional) or oven
Corner punch (optional)

How to make the card:
In the Mixed Bunch rubber stamp set there are 3 large flowers. I stamped a large flower in black ink on white shrink plastic. A different flower in black ink on cream shrink plastic, and the last flower in white ink on black shrink plastic. Remember to stamp on the matt side of the shrink plastic and always use a permanent ink. My example is black and white but if you wanted to add colour you can add it now by colouring in with colour pencils – remember, when shrunk the colour will appear brighter.

Use the matching punch to punch out the flowers, or cut out with scissors leaving a small edge around the stamped image. My example does not have any holes in, but if you were making a key-ring, buttons, or beads you would use a hand held hole punch to punch the holes through the shrink plastic now as this is done before the plastic is shrunk.

Now you are ready to shrink the plastic. There are two options:

Option one: oven bake – follow manufacturer's instructions.

Option two: use a heat gun - to do this you put the plastic on an old wooden chopping board – or a surface that can get very hot. Place a flower on the wooden board image side up, and start to heat with your heat gun. As it heats it will curl up slightly and start to shrink. When it flattens itself out again it is fully shrunk. If it is slightly bent place an acrylic block on top of it for a moment to help it flatten. The image will be very hot. Leave to cool down for a couple of minutes. Repeat for the rest of the flowers.

Tape the flowers on to the black card. Then tape this to the centre of your pre-scored white card and curve the corners with a corner punch. Tie a single knot in some spotty ribbon and stick on the top right hand corner of the black card. Add a pearl to the centre flower to finish off.

***

Watercolour painting   **Trees card**
Beginner

You will need (see Figure 54):
Watercolour paints, and an aqua-painter with water in it
StazOn black ink pad
Watercolour paper
Cream A5 card folded in half and corners curved with a corner punch
Black card, and some spare cream card
Greetings stamp, and matching punches
Lovely as a Tree stamp set by Stampin' Up!

How to make it (see Figure 53):
Ink up the the stamp of a row of trees in StazOn black ink and stamp on to the watercolour paper. Use the aqua-painter in the watercolour paints to paint the colour background. The stamped trees will not run with the permanent ink. I have used blue, blending into brown, and then green beneath the trees. Leave to dry then trim down to size. Mount on to black card.

Figure 53

Figure 54

Position the pre-folded cream card landscape. Ink up the tree stamp in black again and stamp on the bottom of the card so the stamp comes slightly off the bottom of the card. Stamp the trees again until it runs out of ink, if you move the stamp up slightly the paler trees look as if they are in the background. Over-stamping creates a dense background. Repeat the trees so they go all the way across the bottom of the card.

Stick on the painted trees leaving a larger margin at the bottom of the card. Stamp and punch out a greeting in black ink on cream card, mount on black card and stick at the centre of the bottom of the card.

***

Tea light   **Dragonfly tea light**
Some experience

Figure 55   Figure 56

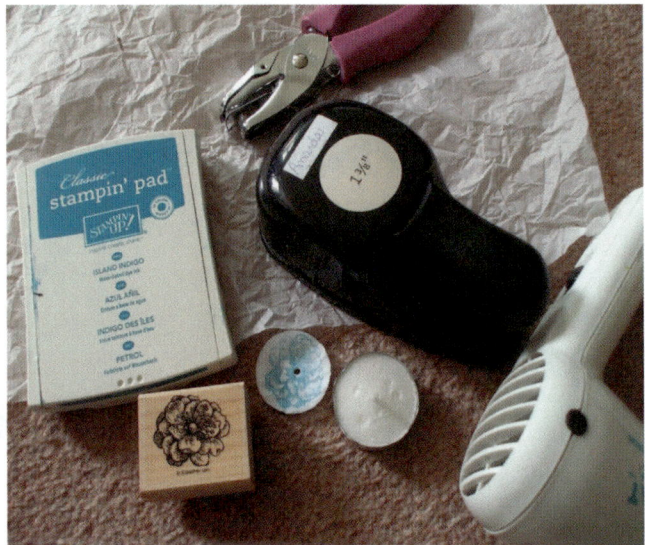

You will need (see Figure 56):
White tissue paper, and a post-it-note
A tea light, and a circle punch (to fit inside the tea light)
Hand held single hole punch, and a turquoise ink pad
Heat gun, and a flower stamp (I used the Everything Eleanor stamp set from Stampin' Up!)

How to make it (see Figure 55):
Ink up the flower stamp in turquoise ink and stamp on to the tissue paper. Put a post-it-note underneath the stamped image and punch out with a circle punch (without the post-it-note the tissue paper will not punch through properly). Use the hand held single hole punch to punch a hole in the centre of the flower. Remove and discard the post-it-note.

Place the stamped image on to the candle by threading the wick through the hole. Use a heat gun to heat fix the tissue paper to the tea light. As the heat gun melts the wax the tissue paper will sink underneath a layer of wax fixing it in place. Take care not to have the heat gun too near the wick or you will discolour it.

When you light the candle, as the wax melts the image will become further beneath the wax so the paper and flame do not come in to contact with each other. Please be aware of candle safety and never leave it unattended.

Why not try: presenting it in a fancy tea light holder, for example a dragonfly, or put a couple together in a poly bag and tie with a ribbon to make small gifts for a dinner party stamped with images appropriate to your theme? I have found that dark and bright coloured inks are the most effective.

***

Figure 57

You will need (see Figure 57):
A white handkerchief
A non-permanent ink pad
Embroidery silk threads in green and purple
Lavender stamp (or similar)

How to make it:
Ink up the lavender stamp in the non-permanent ink (it doesn't matter what colour it is) and stamp it in one corner of the handkerchief. Embroider over the stamped design with the embroidery threads.   I have used French knots for the purple flowers, and a back stitch for the green stems. When you wash the handkerchief the ink will disappear as it is non-permanent leaving you with just the embroidery.

Why not try: stamping on fabric with other items which will be fixed permanently such as acrylic paints using a filled-in stamp with different colours, fabric ink pads specially designed for this purpose, or permanent ink pads that will not wash out?

***

Figure 58

You will need (see Figure 58):
Cotton ribbon
Red ink pad
Flower stamp (I used Best of Flowers from Stampin' Up!)

Selecting the ribbon and ink pads:
When selecting ribbon, you must use a cotton ribbon. Other ribbons can 'bleed' when you put on the ink. Next, let's look at the ink. If you are going to wash the ribbon you must use a permanent ink pad (for example a StazOn ink pad) otherwise the ink will run or wash away completely. If your ribbon is for decoration only and not going to be washed then you can use a non-permanent ink pad.

How to make it:
My ribbon is for decoration only and will not be washed. Therefore I have used a non-permanent red ink pad. Lay out your ribbon on some scrap paper so it is flat. Ink up the stamp in red and start to stamp on to the ribbon. You will find the cotton ribbon ideal for this and fine detail stamps can show up well. I re-inked the stamp each time I stamped it and positioned the stamp right up against the previous image to make a continuous line of flowers all the way along the ribbon.

Why not try: fabric paint instead of ink and heat fix it to the ribbon? You also could use acrylic paint. Why not stamp a matching gift tag and wrapping paper to match the ribbon?

***

Paper daisy
Beginner

Mother's Day card

Figure 59

Figure 60

You will need (see Figure 60):
Pre-folded white card 144 mm square with the corners curved with a corner punch
Bright pink card 8 cm square, and some spare pink card
Silver mirri card 9 cm square, and some spare white card
Paper daisy, and a large silver brad
Bright pink ink pad
Swirls stamp (I used the Everything Eleanor stamp set from Stampin' Up!)
Tiny heart stamp and tiny circle punch
Happy Mother's day stamp, and matching punches
Daisy stamp from the Best of Flowers stamp set from Stampin' Up!
One and a quarter inch scallop circle punch

How to make it (see Figure 59):
Flatten out the paper daisy and ink up the swirls stamp in the pink ink. Stamp the swirls on to the paper daisy and repeat stamping over the daisy, moving the stamp around, until the stamp runs out of ink. Put the silver brad through the hole in the centre of the daisy and flatten out the arms out at the back to hold it in place. Tape the flower on to the pink mount. Then tape this on to the silver mount.

Ink up the swirls stamp in pink ink again and this time stamp on the pre-folded white card. I stamped on each corner changing the direction of the stamp each time. Make sure the image comes off the edges of the card. Tape on the mounted flower in the centre of the card.

On spare white card stamp three daises and a tiny heart in pink ink. Punch out the daises with the scallop circle punch and the heart with a tiny circle punch. Stick the heart on to the centre of the silver brad. Arrange the daises in the bottom left hand corner so they overlap each other, and stick down. I had two flat with tape and raised the top one with foam pads.

Stamp a greeting in pink ink on white card, punch out and tape on to a pink mount. Pad at an angle across the top right hand corner.

***

Faux silk   **Sympathy card**
Some experience

Figure 61   Figure 62

You will need (see Figure 62):
Low tack spray adhesive (high tack is too sticky)
Flower stamp (I used Serene Silhouettes from Stampin' Up!)
Navy ink pad, and navy card
Cream A5 card folded in half, and white tissue paper
Patterned background paper 9 cm x 13.5 cm
Spare white card, and cream card
Greetings stamp with matching punches

How to make it (see Figure 61):
Ink up the flower stamp in the navy ink. We need to use a dark or bright colour for this technique as it will need to show through the tissue paper later on. Stamp the flower on to the spare white card. Trim down to size, then cut some tissue paper slightly larger than it.

You need to work in a well ventilated area and place your stamped flower on to some newspaper. Scrunch up the tissue paper and open it out again. Spray the flower with the spray adhesive and then press the tissue paper on top. Press it down flat. The creases in the tissue paper add to the silk effect. Also, some spray adhesives can 'yellow' the image and this can make it look distressed. Leave to dry (don't worry if any of it sticks to the newspaper as this can be cut off later).

When dry remove it from the newspaper and trim around the card image, chopping off the excess tissue paper. Mount on to navy card. Mount on to the centre of the patterned paper, then mount this on to some navy card. Stick the whole thing on to the pre-folded cream card.

Stamp a greeting in navy ink on spare cream card, punch out and stick on to a mount. Attach to the card in the top right hand corner.

Why not try: this technique but stamping an outline in black ink and colouring in with bright colour pens?

***

Core card (rubbing)
Beginner

Three Christmas trees card

What is core card?
Core card is great fun to use. It is made up of 3 parts (like a sandwich). It has two outer layers, and an inner layer which is a paler colour. The core card is also slightly textured. It can be torn to expose the inner colour, it can be scrunched up and then opened out and sanded down to make an interesting background, it can be embossed through an embossing machine and then sanded to make interesting patterns.

Figure 63

Figure 64

You will need (see Figure 64):
Green core card
Sanding block with very fine sand paper
Green ink pad, and white ink pad
Patterned papers, and spare green card
Black card, and narrow black ribbon
White square pre-folded 144 mm card, and spare white card
A Christmas tree stamp (I used Scentsational Season stamp set from Stampin' Up!)
Silver star, and glitter glue
A Christmas greeting and matching punches

How to make it (see Figure 63):
Position the green core card so it is texture side up. Because it is textured it is not that easy to stamp on to, so we are going to use our stamp a different way. The stamp we want to use must be a very distinctive shape, so a Christmas tree is ideal. It must also be a filled-in stamp (solid stamp).

Place your stamp rubber side up underneath the core card. Hold the card still with one hand and use the sanding block to rub over the stamp with the other. The sander will wear away the top layer of the core card where the stamp is exposing the paler colour. The shape of the tree should start to appear. When the tree is fully showing remove the core card and blow away the dust.

On spare white card stamp the tree in green ink and clean the stamp. On spare green card stamp the tree in white ink. Trim all 3 trees down to 5 cm x 6 cm. Mount them all on black card and trim down to size.

Cut a patterned piece of paper to 12.5 cm square. Stick on to a black mount and stick on to the pre-folded white card. Cut 2 pieces of different patterned paper to 5 cm x 6 cm and mount them on to black card.

Arrange the mounted patterned papers on to the card (as in Figure 63), and then the trees on the top. Stick down with tape, apart from the central tree which I padded. Stamp and punch out a greeting and a mount, then tape it in the bottom left hand corner of the card. Add a star, bow, and silver glitter glue (one item per tree) to finish off.

***

Stamping on air-drying clay   **Reindeer decoration**
Beginner

You will need (see Figure 66):
Air-drying white clay, and some red glitter glue
Reindeer stamp (I used the Joyous Celebrations stamp set from Stampin' Up!)
Green ink pad, and a finger dauber
Brown ink pad, and some brown ribbon
Brayer (optional), and a fine tip black pen

Figure 65

Figure 66

How to make it (see Figure 65):

Take a small piece of clay and roll it out flat using a brayer (like a rolling pin). Ink up the reindeer in brown ink and press on to the clay (but not too hard or you may get some marks from the edge of the stamp). Put some red glitter glue on the nose. Leave to dry for 24 hours.

When dry, trim down with scissors to make an oval shape. Punch through a hole (not too close to the edge) and thread through some ribbon. Use the finger dauber in the green ink pad to daub all around the deer to make the green background, Finally, finish by dotting an eye with the fine tip black pen. I have left my decoration as it is, but you could varnish it if you wanted it to shine.

Why not try: colouring the clay with a few drops of coloured ink from the ink-refills (designed to top up your coloured ink pads) before moulding or stamping on to the clay?

***

Heat 'n' Stick Powder to add glitter to your stamping   **Christmas tree card**
Some experience

Figure 67   Figure 68

You will need (see Figure 68):
Square 5" x 5" pre-folded white card, and spare white card
Red card, and red ribbon
Versamark ink pad, and a black ink pad
Evergreen Stamp Set from Stampin' Up!, and some patterned paper
Heat & Stick Powder from Stampin' Up!, and a heat gun
Dazzling Diamonds glitter from Stampin' Up! (or similar transparent glitter)
Felt tip pens in different shades of green
Clips with green bows on (available from Stampin' Up!)

How to make it (see Figure 67):
Ink up the outline Christmas tree stamp from the Evergreen Stamp set in black ink and stamp on to some spare white card. Trim down to size. Colour in the tree using the different shades of green pens.

Place it on to some scrap paper and tap the Versamark ink pad over the top of your image to cover it in ink. Place your image on to some clean scrap paper and pour over some heat & stick powder. Tap away the excess powder and pour it back into the pot. Use your heat gun to melt the powder. As it melts the image will become clearer. Take care as it is now hot and sticky. Next pour on some glitter, tip away the excess glitter and pour it back in the pot. Use your heat gun to heat the glitter to fix it. It is essential to use a transparent glitter so that we can see the Christmas tree underneath the glitter. As the glitter is heated it will twinkle. When it stops twinkling the glitter has been heat fixed to the card. This is a good way of adding some sparkle to your card safe in the knowledge that the glitter will not fall off.

Mount the image on to some patterned paper and trim down to size. Place a clip with a green bow on it at the top, and then mount this at an angle on to some red card. Stamp the words in black ink on white card and mount on the patterned paper. Trim to size.

Place a large red ribbon all the way around the card and tie with a knot at the front of the card (make sure the ribbon is flat and does not twist inside the card). Trim the ribbon ends at an angle with some sharp scissors. Slide the knot down towards the bottom of the card.

Tape the mounted tree on to the right hand side of the card. I also curved the corners using a corner punch on the right hand side of the card only. Pad on the words in the top left hand corner so they overlap the ribbon and also some of the red card.

***

Heat embossing to make a resist
Some experience

Feather bookmark

Figure 69

Figure 70

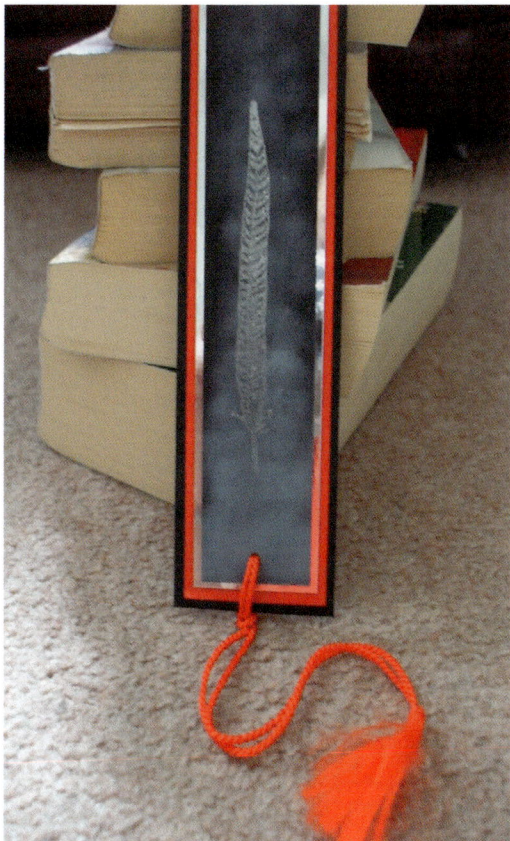

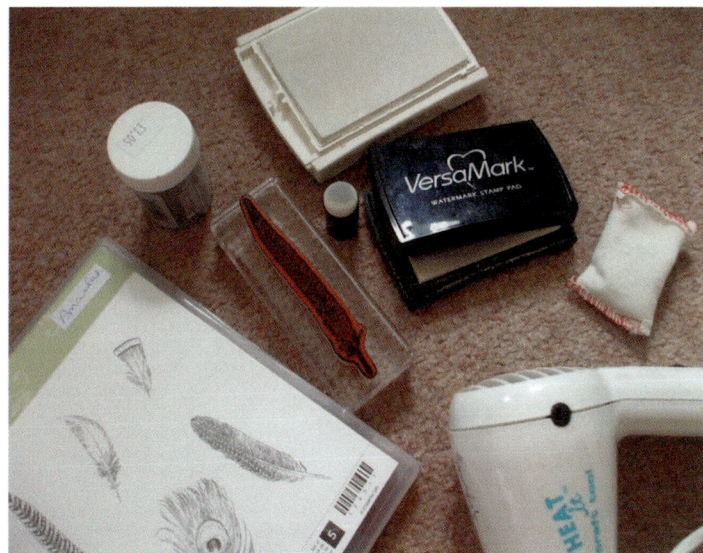

You will need (see Figure 70):
Card in black and red
Silver mirri card
A red tassel, and a finger dauber

Versamark ink pad, and a white ink pad
Silver embossing powder
Feather stamp (I used Fine Feathers stamp set from Stampin Up!)
Heat gun, and embossing buddy (anti-static pad)
Hand-held single hole punch

How to make it (see Figure 69):
Rub over the black card with the anti-static pad. Ink up the feather stamp in Versamark ink. This is a clear sticky ink. Stamp on to the black card. Sprinkle the silver embossing powder on top of the impression before the ink dries. Carefully tip away the excess embossing powder taking care not to knock off any powder that is stuck to the feather impression. The anti-static pad will prevent the powder from sticking on other parts of the black card.

Lay your card on a surface that you can use with a heat gun (for example an old wooden chopping board). Use the heat gun to melt the embossing powder so that it is heat fixed to the card. When using a heat gun take care not to over-melt the powder or it will lose its shine and become dull, or to under-melt the powder which will not stick and fall off. You should be able to see the powder melt as the heat begins to work as it slightly changes colour. The card will become hot so use a kebab stick or similar to hold the card in place. Leave for a few minutes to cool down. Trim down the card to a long narrow strip, 3.5 cm x 16.5 cm.

Place your finger dauber on the white ink pad and dab on some white colour over the feather. I have concentrated the colour at the bottom of the card and made it less so as I come further up the card. The silver feather will disappear underneath the white ink, so take a piece of tissue and rub over the white ink. Where the ink is on top of the silver embossing it will wipe away exposing the silver feather underneath. The embossing acts as a resistance.

Mount this on to some silver mirri card, then on to red card, and finally on to some black card. Use a hand-held single hole punch to punch a hole at the bottom centre of the book mark and thread through a red tassel.

***

Heat embossing using metallic or coloured powders   **Embossed picture**
Some experience

You will need:
A picture frame
Some coloured card (I used pink)
Silver embossing powder
Heat gun
Versamark ink pad
Anti-static pad, and a fine dry paint brush
A large patterned stamp (I used one from Stampin' Up!)

How to make it (see Figure 71):

Rub over the pink card with the anti-static pad. Ink up the stamp with the Versamark ink pad taking care to cover all the stamp. Stamp on to the pink card and quickly pour on the silver embossing powder before the ink dries. Tip away the excess powder. Use the dry paintbrush to carefully remove any patches of powder where it is not required, taking care not to knock away any powder that you do.

Figure 71

Carefully lay your card on a surface that you can use with a heat gun (for example an old wooden chopping board). Use the heat gun to melt the embossing powder so that it is heat fixed to the card. When using a heat gun take care not to over-melt the powder or it will lose its shine and become dull, or to under-melt the powder which will not stick and fall off. You should be able to see the powder melt as the heat begins to work. The card will become hot so use a kebab stick or similar to hold the card in place. Leave for a few minutes to cool down.

Remove the glass from the picture frame and place over the top of your stamped image, so that the image is in the centre. Draw around the glass with a pencil and cut out. The stamped image should now fit perfectly inside your picture frame.

Why not try: using different coloured card with different coloured powders, making your own coloured powders by mixing some coloured chalks in with some clear embossing powder, or sprinkling some gold and some silver patches on your image (one at a time so you don't mix your powders) so you have a multi-coloured embossed image? If your frame has a mount inside, why not stamp on the mount to decorate that as well?

***

Figure 72   Figure 73

You will need (see Figure 73):
Cream A5 card folded in half and the corners curved with a corner punch
Dark red patterned strip of paper, and light coloured patterned paper (to stamp on top of)
Green and red ink pads, and a Versamark ink pad
Gold peel off lines, and a one inch circle punch
Greetings stamp and matching punches
Mixed Bunch stamp set from Stampin' Up!
Joyous Celebrations stamp set from Stampin' Up!
Clear embossing powder and a heat gun

How to make it (see Figure 72):
Position your pre-folded cream card landscape and lay the patterned strip of paper across it near the bottom. Tape it down and cut off any excess paper at either end.

Ink up the largest flower circle stamp from the Mixed Bunch stamp set in red. Stamp 3 images on to the paler coloured patterned paper, making sure that you re-ink the stamp between each impression. Clean the stamp and then stamp 2 images in green ink on to the same patterned paper, again re-inking the stamp between each impression. Punch out all of the flowers with the circle punch.

Place a circle directly on the Versamark pad so the stamped image side of the circle is sticky. Remove the circle from the pad and place on some scrap paper. Sprinkle on clear embossing powder, tip off the excess power, then heat fix with a heat gun. You will need to use a kebab stick to hold the circles still while you heat them, and then leave them for a few minutes to cool down. Repeat for all of the circles. You should now have shiny patterned Christmas baubles.

Arrange the baubles across the cream card, alternating between red and green. Remove the first red bauble and ink up the bow stamp from the Joyous Celebrations stamp set with green ink. Stamp on to the card and then pad the bauble directly below it. Repeat this for all the baubles, so the green baubles have red bows and vice versa.

Gently lay on gold peel off lines from the top of the bows to the top of the card. When happy that they are straight press them down in place and trim off the excess.

Stamp a greeting in red ink on spare cream card. Punch out and stick on to a patterned paper mount, then stick this on to red card and trim down to size. Pad in the top left hand corner.

**

Chapter 7 Kiss stamping

Kiss stamping is when you have 2 different stamps and press them together to create different effects. One of them must be a filled-in stamp (a solid stamp) and the other must be an outline stamp or a patterned stamp. You can get stamps specially designed to go together for this purpose, but also random stamps used together for kiss stamping can look just as effective.

I have a butterflies stamp set from Stampin' Up! (Papillon Potpourri) which contains a filled-in butterfly (solid stamp) and some patterned butterflies the same size, so these stamps work very well for kiss stamping. I have made all of my examples using these stamps.

Figure 74

Direct stamp to stamp
Beginner

Butterflies in a row card

Figure 75

Figure 76

You will need (see Figure 76):
Fancy fan embossing folder, and embossing machine
White A5 card folded in half, and some spare white card

Corner punch, and white ribbon
Turquoise and pink ink pads
Turquoise and pink card
Butterflies stamp set and matching butterfly punch
Thank you stamp and punches for mounting (I used scalloped oval, large oval and fancy tag punches)

How to make it (see Figure 75):
Ink up the solid butterfly stamp in pink ink. Ink up the patterned butterfly stamp in turquoise ink. Press the two stamps together taking care to line them up (this part is the kissing – see Figure 74). Put the patterned stamp to one side. Stamp the solid stamp on to some spare white card. You should be able to see the turquoise detail of the pattern on top of a pink background. Punch out with the butterfly punch. Repeat to make 5 butterflies. Clean the stamps after each use so that you don't contaminate the ink pads.

Cut some white card 14 cm x 6.5 cm. Place inside the fancy fan embossing folder making sure it is straight and emboss through an embossing machine.

Position the embossed white card landscape. Cut a narrow strip of turquoise and pink card. Place the pink strip underneath the embossed white card so you only see a small edge at the top. Stick in place and cut off any excess card showing on the left and right hand sides. Do this again with the turquoise card so it is slightly above the pink card.

Cut two pieces of white ribbon. Tape one end to the back of the embossed white card beneath the pink strip at one side. Tape the second piece of ribbon to the other side, bring the two ends to the front of the card and tie a knot or a bow towards the left hand side. Tape the whole thing to the bottom of the white folded card. Use the corner punch to punch all four corners.

Arrange the butterflies across the top of the card so they are above the coloured strips. Stick down in place. Punch out a butterfly in spare turquoise and pink card. Stick the butterflies in the bottom left hand corner.

Stamp a greeting in turquoise ink on to some spare white card and punch out with the scalloped oval punch. Stick this in turn on to a turquoise oval, and then on to pink card punched out with the fancy tag punch. Tape the greeting in place on to the card.

***

Twisted kiss stamping   **Purple thank you card**
Some experience

You will need (see Figure 78):
Purple A5 card folded in half and the corners curved with a corner punch
White card 6 cm x 10.5 cm, and spare white card
White, green and purple ink pads
Brush marker pens in pale pink, purple and green
Thank you greetings stamp from the Banners stamp set (from Stampin Up!)
Butterflies stamp set and matching butterfly punch
Flower stamp from the Serene Silhouettes stamp set (from Stampin Up!)

Figure 77   Figure 78

How to make it (see Figure 77):
Ink up the filled-in butterfly stamp in green ink. Ink up the patterned butterfly stamp in purple ink. Press the two stamps together (this part is the kissing – see Figure 74). Keep the solid stamp still, and twist the patterned stamp round approximately ninety degrees (this part is the twisting). Separate the stamps.

Put the patterned stamp to one side. Stamp the solid stamp on to some spare white card. You should be able to see an abstract pattern of purple and green. Punch out the butterfly using the matching punch. Make three butterflies this way (take care to clean the stamps each time between use so that you do not contaminate your ink pads).

Place your purple pre-folded card landscape. Place the rectangle of white card portrait. Use brush marker pens (as described in Chapter 1) to colour directly on to the stamp. Start with the pink for the flowers, then the purple at the centres of the flowers, and finally the rest of the leaves and grass in green. 'Huff' on to the stamp and then stamp on to the white card so that the bottom of the stamp comes slightly off the bottom of the white card (this is so the flower is not in mid-air). Tape this on to the purple card approx 1 cm in from the left hand side. Clean and dry the flower stamp.

Ink up the flowers stamp in white ink and stamp towards the right hand side of the purple card, also stamping it so that it slightly comes off the bottom of the stamp (to keep level with the other flower). Arrange the butterflies on the card and stick down. Stamp a greeting in purple ink on white card and cut out. Stick in the centre of the card at the top so it overlaps both the white and purple card.

***

Reverse kiss stamping
Beginner

Purple butterflies on white flower

Figure 79

Figure 80

You will need (see Figure 80):
Butterflies stamp set and matching butterfly punch
White A5 card and some spare white card
A5 piece of vellum
White sheer spotty ribbon
Flowers embossing folder and embossing machine
Self-adhesive pearls, and white liquid pearls
A5 purple card and some spare purple card
Greeting stamp (from the Banners stamp set by Stampin' Up!)

How to make it (see Figure 79):
Ink up the filled-in butterfly stamp with purple ink. Do not put any ink on the patterned butterfly stamp as this time we are removing ink instead of adding it. Press the two stamps together so that they kiss, taking care to line them up (see Figure 74). Remove the pattern stamp and put to one side. Stamp the filled-in stamp on to some spare white card. You should be able to see the pattern showing pale purple against a darker purple background. Punch out the butterfly using the butterfly punch. Repeat to make three butterflies. Clean and dry the patterned stamp each time you use it to ensure that each time you are removing ink from the solid stamp (and not putting any ink back on).

Place the vellum inside the flowers embossing folder so that the flowers are at the right hand side and the vellum is landscape, then emboss through an embossing machine. Fold the vellum in half to make a sleeve so the flowers are at the front right hand side of the sleeve.

Take the purple A5 card and slice a few millimetres off one of the short sides. Fold in half. Slip this card inside the folded vellum sleeve. Tie some white spotty ribbon all away around the fold of the card and tie a knot or bow at the front, making sure the ribbon does not twist inside the card. Tie it tight to keep the vellum sleeve and purple card together (but not so tight that the card begins to bend).

Punch out a couple of butterflies from spare white card. Arrange all the butterflies on the card and stick down. You can lift up the vellum and put some glue underneath the butterflies so that the vellum sticks to the purple card underneath to help keep the card together. The glue will not show because it is underneath the butterflies. Add some self-adhesive pearls to the centres of the white butterflies.

Stamp a greeting in purple ink, cut out and stick on to a punched out purple background tag shape. Pad in place on the top left hand corner of the card.

***

Stamping-off on embossed card (for a kiss stamped effect)
Beginner

Butterflies get well card

Figure 81

Figure 82

This card looks as if the butterflies have been kiss stamped but in fact they have been made using a stamping-off technique instead. The results are very similar.

You will need (see Figure 82):
Papillon Potpouri stamp set from Stampin' Up!, and matching butterfly punch
Basket weave embossing folder and an embossing machine
Large scallop circle punch (mine is two and three eighths of an inch)
Patterned paper
Some spare white card
Three different coloured ink pads to match your papers (I used pale pink, pale blue and green)
White A5 card folded in half and the corners curved with a corner punch
3D foam pads
Get well wishes stamp and matching punch, and a tag punch for a mount

How to make it (see Figure 81):
Cut some white card to 9.5 cm x 13.5 cm and place inside the basket weave embossing folder taking care to line it up straight, and emboss through your embossing machine.

Insert the top of the embossed card into the scallop circle punch as far as it will go. Make sure the sides are evenly spaced on the left and right, then punch out. Put the scallop circle to one side so we can use it later.

Place the textured card on to the pre-folded white card in the centre and draw around the aperture with a pencil. Remove the embossed card. Cut some patterned paper so that it is larger than the scallop circle and stick it on to the white card so that it completely covers the pencil scallop outline. Put foam pads on the back of the embossed white card and reposition back on to the card and stick down. You should be able to see the patterned paper through the aperture.

Ink up the filled-in butterfly from the stamp set in pale pink ink. Stamp it on to the embossed scallop circle, and then stamp it on to some spare white card. This technique is called 'stamping-off'. You should have a pink butterfly impression with a basket weave pattern. Punch it out with the butterfly punch. Repeat to make a total of three butterflies in pale pink, pale blue and green. Arrange the butterflies around the aperture so they go partly over the edges and glue in place. Stamp a greeting in green ink on to white card and punch out. Punch out a mount in patterned paper and stick at the bottom of the card.

***

Sometimes stamps are made with all sorts of accessories designed specifically to use with them. In this chapter we will look at stamps that have matching embossing folders, background papers and punches.

Wildflower Meadow stamp with matching embossing folder   **Blue flower card**
Some experience

Figure 83   Figure 84

This project involves a combination of techniques.

To make it you will need (see Figure 84):
Wildflower Meadow stamp and matching embossing folder (from Stampin Up!)
An embossing machine (eg Sizzex, Cuttlebug or similar)
Brush marker pens in pale blue, turquoise and green
Turquoise ink pad, and a brayer
White A5 card folded in half for your actual card, and some spare white card.
Corner punch (optional)

How to make it (see Figure 83):
Curve the corners with a corner punch of your folded white card (optional).

Use the brush marker pens directly on to the Wildflower Meadow stamp. Start with the lightest colour (pale blue) and colour in the flowers. Use the thicker end of the pen to brush the colour on to the stamp. Then go in with the green on the leaves and stems (the medium colour). Finally, use the darkest colour (turquoise) to colour in the centres of the flowers. Next, huff on to the stamp to moisten the areas of the pens which are starting to dry. Then stamp on to some spare white card, pressing firmly. Wipe the stamp clean.

Next, open up your Wildflower Meadow embossing folder. We are going to brayer ink from the turquoise ink pad directly on to the embossing folder. To do this you are going to put colour on to the side where you can see the logo through the plastic (the embossing area is recessed). Roll your brayer continuously in the same direction across your ink pad to load it fully with ink and then roll the brayer on to the embossing folder, again continuously in the same direction to get maximum coverage of ink. Cover the one side with ink. If you get any ink in the recessed area which should remain clear you can carefully wipe it off with a damp tissue.

Place the stamped image inside the matching Wildflower Meadow embossing folder so that the logo is on the top and the stamped image is face up. Line up the flowers and leaves so they are inside the recessed areas. Emboss through your embossing machine. Clean your embossing folder and brayer by washing them in water. **Do this straight away or you could stain them.**

Trim the image down to size so it will fit on the front of your white card and curve the corners (optional). Tape on to the front of the folded card.

I liked this card just as it is, but you can always add greetings, bows, glitter in the centre of the flowers, etc.

***

Mosaic Madness with punch and papers   **Christmas baubles card**
Some experience

This example uses many items that co-ordinate with each other. I used Stampin' Up! products.

You will need (see Figure 86):
Mosaic Madness stamp set and matching punch
Diagonally striped papers and matching embossing folder
Silver embellishments: button, bow and gem stone
Greetings stamp and matching punch, with larger punch for mount
Ink pad to match one of the colours in the patterned paper (I used Bermuda Bay)
Silver peel off lines
5" x 7" pre-scored white card with the corners curved
10 cm x 14 cm white card and some spare white card
Bermuda Bay card
One and three quarters of an inch circle punch, and a slightly smaller circle punch

How to make it (see Figure 85):
Ink up one of the mosaic stamps in the Bermuda Bay ink and randomly stamp all around the outside edge of the front of the pre-folded white card. Re-ink the stamp each time you use it and take the impressions off the side of the card. Vary the direction of the stamp to create an interesting and bright background to your card.

Figure 85   Figure 86

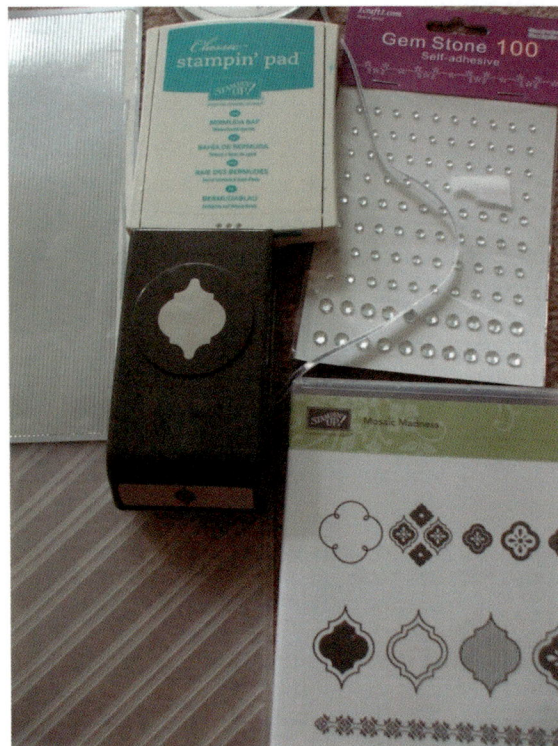

Punch out a mosaic out of spare white card (not too close to the edge). Discard the shape as we are going to use the aperture only. Place the circle punch over the aperture (if you hold your circle punch upside down you can line up the mosaic exactly in the centre of the circle. Punch out the circle. Insert the circle into the diagonal embossing folder and emboss through an embossing machine. Punch out a smaller circle from the diagonal patterned paper. Place the larger circle on top so that the stripes are all going in the same direction and pad in place. Repeat to make a total of three baubles.

Insert the 10 cm x 14 cm white card into the diagonal embossing folder and emboss through an embossing machine. Place the three baubles on top (do not stick down yet) so they are in line with the diagonal pattern on the white background. Gently lay down silver peel-off lines where the strings for the baubles will go. If they are not straight carefully lift them up and re-align them. Trim off the ends at the top. Stick down the baubles.

Mount the whole thing on to the Bermuda Bay card and trim down to make a mount. Stick this on to the centre of the pre-folded card.

Decorate the centres of the baubles with silver embellishments. I have used a bow, button and a gem stone. Stamp and punch out a greeting in matching ink, and mount on matching card. Pad across the bottom right hand corner (or wherever you think there is a gap).

**

Figure 87   Figure 88

It can be fun to experiment with stamps and folders that are not designed to go together as well as those that do.

You will need (see Figure 88):
Wildflower Meadow stamp (from Stampin' Up!) or a large flower stamp
White ink pad, and a glue stick
Hexagons embossing folder and embossing machine
Pre-folded 5" x 7" white card with the corners curved with a corner punch
Spare white and turquoise card
Happy Birthday stamp with matching punch (mine was from Stampin' Up!)
Spotty white ribbon

How to make it (see Figure 87):
Cut some white card to fit inside the hexagon embossing folder and emboss through your embossing machine.

Ink up the Wildflower Meadow stamp in white ink and stamp on to the turquoise card. Press firmly.

When the ink is dry insert into the hexagon embossing folder and emboss through the machine.

The stamped coloured hexagons are cut out and stuck on to the white hexagon background. To do this I suggest you cut a strip at a time. Each time you cut out a hexagon immediately place it on the white hexagon background, otherwise it is very easy to end up with a lot of pieces and very difficult to find where they all go. Stick them down with a glue stick.

Trim down the sides neatly and mount on to white card. Then mount this on to some turquoise card, and stick the whole thing on to the white pre-folded card. I left a larger margin at the bottom.

Stamp a greeting in white ink on spare turquoise card and punch out. Pad in the centre of the bottom of the card. Add a white spotty bow in the top left hand corner.

***

Builder stamp
Some experience

Figure 89

Birthday cake card

Figure 90

When using builder stamps we really notice the difference between wood and clear stamps. When using a clear mount stamp we can see through the acrylic block so we can fairly accurately line up the stamps when building up our images. We are not able to do this with a wood mount stamp so by using a stamp-a-ma-jig we can make the images line up precisely. The stamp-a-ma-jig is also very useful for lining up greetings so they are straight when stamping directly on to the card.

How to use a stamp-a-ma-jig (from Stampin' Up!):
A stamp-a-ma-jig consists of two parts: an acetate imaging sheet, and the black stamp-a-ma-jig. Place the acetate imaging sheet texture side up in the corner of the black stamp-a-ma-jig. Ink up your stamp with a non-permanent ink and align in the corner, and stamp on to the imaging sheet.

Place the imaging sheet where you intend to stamp. Line up the stamp-a-ma-jig with the imaging sheet then carefully remove the imaging sheet. Re-ink your stamp and align with the stamp-a-ma-jig to get your image in precisely the right place. When finished wipe the imaging sheet clean.

You will need (see Figure 90): (all these items are from Stampin' Up!)
Make a Cake builder stamp set (mine is a wooden stamp set, so I also need a stamp-a-ma-jig)
Blue and pink brush marker pens
White A5 card, plus some spare white card
Pink and blue card, and a greetings stamp
Patterned paper (mine matches the stamps) 9 cm x 13.5 cm

How to make it (see Figure 89):
Use a brush marker pen to colour pink ink on the stamp which is the bottom of the cake, and then use the blue pen for the stand. Stamp near the bottom of some white card. Use brush marker pens to colour on the stamp with the next two tiers on, but this time use a stamp-a-ma-jig (as described above) to line up precisely where to stamp. Repeat for the flags, and the butterflies. When finished trim down the white card to size. Mount on pink card and trim to size.

Stick the patterned paper on to a blue mount and trim down to size. Fold the A5 white card in half and stick the mounted paper on the front. Stick on the mounted cake in the centre. Use brush marker pens to colour on to the greetings stamp (I used 2 different colours) and stamp on to some spare white card, cut out and stick across the top left hand corner of the card.

***

Framelits   **Christmas gift bag with framelit tag**
Beginner

You will need (see Figure 92):
Paper gift bag, and some spare white card
Ink pads in green, brown, red and yellow
Scentsational Stamps and matching framelits from Stampin' Up!,
An embossing machine
Assortment of ribbons in green, brown, red and yellow
Low tack masking tap, a single hand held hole punch

Figure 91   Figure 92

How to make it (see Figure 91):

Start with the largest stamp and ink up in your first colour (I started with red mugs). Stamp on to the front of the bag, including off the edges of the bag. Re-ink each time you stamp to get a strong colour. Leave plenty of space between the images so we have plenty of room for the other stamps (you can always add more later on).

Repeat using the next largest stamp in your next colour, and so on, until you are left with the star. You can use the smallest stamp as a fill-in for any gaps you may have. I decorated the front of the bag only but you can also do the back if you wish.

On spare white card stamp the brown gingerbread man. I used a framelit to die cut him to make a gift tag. Place the framelit on top of the gingerbread man cutting edge down, and use the masking tape to keep it in position. Run it though your embossing machine to die cut it. I have punched a hole and threaded through some ribbon and tied it to the handle. If this is too small for you to write on you could stick him on to some larger white card first. Finish off decorating the gift bag by tying lots of scraps of co-ordinating ribbons around the handles.

***

Acrylic block printing   **Shells card**
Beginner

Figure 93   Figure 94

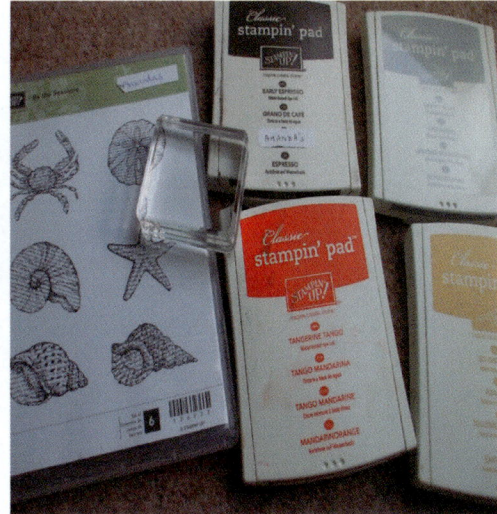

You will need (see Figure 94):
A small acrylic block (that you use with clear stamps), mine was 5 cm x 4.5 cm
Dark brown ink pad and several coloured ink pads in yellows, light browns, greys and orange
Shell stamp set (I used By the Seashore from Stampin' Up!)
Brown card to mount
White square pre-folded card 144 mm, and some spare white card

How to make it (see Figure 93):
Place the acrylic block directly on top of one of the coloured ink pads and then press down on the spare white card. Carefully remove the block and you should have a colour rectangle. It doesn't matter if the impression is not perfect (it almost always isn't anyway), and it adds to the distressed effect. In fact I think the card looks better like this. Wipe clean and dry the acrylic block. Ink it up in another colour and print again right up against (or slightly overlapping) the previous impression. Continue until you have a square block of nine colours. You can repeat colours so long as they are not next to each other. Do not use the dark brown ink to make a block.

Ink up a shell in the dark brown ink and stamp on to one of the blocks. Repeat with another shell in another block, and so on. You will need to use some of the stamps more than once so make sure that you do not end up with two shells next to each other. Trim down the decorated card to 12 cms square. It doesn't matter if you slice through some of the shells to do this (I have on my example). Mount on to the dark brown card, trim to size and mount on to the pre-folded square white card.

***

Figure 95

Figure 96

You will need (see Figure 96):
Acrylic block (or an imaging sheet from a stamp-a-ma-jig by Stampin' Up!)
Zoo Review stamp set
Non-permanent black and white ink pads
Greetings stamp, and a curly label punch
Blue A5 card folded in half and the corners curved with a corner punch
Spare blue card, and some white card
Top Note die, and die cutting machine
Narrow blue ribbon, and white liquid pearls
Water-colour paints, and an aqua-painter with water in it

How to make it (see Figure 95):
Place the white card on top of the top note die and cut through an embossing machine. Ink up the polar bear stamp in black ink and stamp on the top note near the right hand side, not too close to the bottom (leaving room for the reflection).

You can either use an acrylic block or the imaging sheet from a stamp-a-ma-jig to make the reflection. Whether you are using an acrylic block or an imaging sheet the instructions are exactly the same. Ink up the polar bear stamp in black ink and stamp on to the acrylic block (or the smooth side of the imaging sheet). You should now have the image on the block (or imaging sheet). Turn it over so the ink is now underneath. Because they are transparent you can line up the reflection beneath the polar bear that you have stamped, then press down the acrylic block (or imaging sheet) very firmly. The ink will then transfer on to the card and there you have your reflection. If your reflection is not perfect I don't think this matters too much, as some reflections are not always very clear in real life, the reflection will also be paler. Wipe clean your acrylic block or imaging sheet (we have used a non-permanent ink pad so we can clean them; a permanent ink would not clean off).

Next we add some water-colour. As we did not use a permanent ink pad this needs to be done quite carefully so the ink doesn't bleed. Paint on some very pale blue as a series of lines that do not quite touch the stamping. The colour is not a solid block, it is deliberately very patchy as it is ice reflecting the sky. Leave to dry.

Stamp a greeting in white ink on spare blue card and punch out with the curly label punch. Lay two strips of ribbon towards the left hand side of the top note so they cross over in the middle and use a small piece of tape to hold them down (the tape is hidden later by the greeting). Turn over the top note and tape down the ribbon ends on the back. Tape the whole thing on to the blue pre-folded card. Tape or pad on the greeting to hide your tape. Finish off with white liquid pearls dotted on the blue card as snow.

***

I hope you try some of these projects, and enjoy your crafting.

Printed in Great Britain
by Amazon.co.uk, Ltd.,
Marston Gate.